THE BEDFORD SERIES IN HISTORY AND CULTURE

The U.S. War with Mexico

A Brief History with Documents

Related Titles in
THE BEDFORD SERIES IN HISTORY AND CULTURE
Advisory Editors: Lynn Hunt, *University of California, Los Angeles*
David W. Blight, *Yale University*
Bonnie G. Smith, *Rutgers University*
Natalie Zemon Davis, *Princeton University*
Ernest R. May, *Harvard University*

Victors and Vanquished: Spanish and Nahua Views of the Conquest of Mexico
Edited with an Introduction by Stuart B. Schwartz, *Yale University*

Envisioning America: English Plans for the Colonization of North America, 1580–1640
Edited with an Introduction by Peter C. Mancall, *University of Southern California*

THE LANCASTER TREATY OF 1744 *with Related Documents*
James H. Merrell, *Vassar College*

The World Turned Upside Down: Indian Voices from Early America
Edited with an Introduction by Colin G. Calloway, *Dartmouth College*

The Lewis and Clark Expedition: Selections from the Journals, Arranged by Topic
Edited with an Introduction by Gunther Barth, *University of California, Berkeley*

The Cherokee Removal: A Brief History with Documents, Second Edition
Theda Perdue and Michael D. Green, *University of North Carolina at Chapel Hill*

John Brown's Raid on Harpers Ferry: A Brief History with Documents
Jonathan Earle, *University of Kansas*

Abraham Lincoln, Slavery, and the Civil War: Selected Writings and Speeches
Edited by Michael P. Johnson, *Johns Hopkins University*

Our Hearts Fell to the Ground: Plains Indian Views of How the West Was Lost
Edited with an Introduction by Colin G. Calloway, *Dartmouth College*

César Chávez: A Brief Biography with Documents
Edited with an Introduction by Richard W. Etulain, *University of New Mexico*

THE BEDFORD SERIES IN HISTORY AND CULTURE

The U.S. War with Mexico

A Brief History with Documents

Ernesto Chávez

University of Texas at El Paso

BEDFORD/ST. MARTIN'S   Boston ♦ New York

To Norris Hundley Jr.

For Bedford/St. Martin's

Publisher for History: Mary Dougherty
Director for Development: Jane Knetzger
Developmental Editor: Debra Michals
Editorial Assistants: Laurel Damashek, Katherine Flynn
Senior Production Supervisor: Nancy J. Myers
Production Associate: Sarah Ulicny
Executive Marketing Manager: Jenna Bookin Barry
Project Management: Books By Design, Inc.
Text Design: Claire Seng-Niemoeller
Index: Books By Design, Inc.
Cover Design: Donna Lee Dennison
Cover Art: *Scott's Entrance into Mexico City, September 14, 1847* (detail) by Carl Nebel. Published in George Wilkins Kendall, *The War Between the United States and Mexico Illustrated*. Appleton & Co., N.Y., 1851. Courtesy, Special Collections, The University of Texas at Arlington Library, Arlington, Texas.
Composition: Stratford/TexTech
Printing and Binding: RR Donnelley & Sons Company

President: Joan E. Feinberg
Editorial Director: Denise B. Wydra
Director of Marketing: Karen Melton Soeltz
Director of Editing, Design, and Production: Marcia Cohen
Manager, Publishing Services: Emily Berleth

Library of Congress Control Number: 2007933166

For information, write: Bedford/St. Martin's, 75 Arlington Street, Boston, MA 02116 (617-399-4000)

ISBN-10: 0-312-24921-7
ISBN-13: 978-0-312-24921-2

Acknowledgments

Acknowledgments and copyrights are continued at the back of the book on page 159, which constitutes an extension of the copyright page.

Foreword

The Bedford Series in History and Culture is designed so that readers can study the past as historians do.

The historian's first task is finding the evidence. Documents, letters, memoirs, interviews, pictures, movies, novels, or poems can provide facts and clues. Then the historian questions and compares the sources. There is more to do than in a courtroom, for hearsay evidence is welcome, and the historian is usually looking for answers beyond act and motive. Different views of an event may be as important as a single verdict. How a story is told may yield as much information as what it says.

Along the way the historian seeks help from other historians and perhaps from specialists in other disciplines. Finally, it is time to write, to decide on an interpretation and how to arrange the evidence for readers.

Each book in this series contains an important historical document or group of documents, each document a witness from the past and open to interpretation in different ways. The documents are combined with some element of historical narrative—an introduction or a biographical essay, for example—that provides students with an analysis of the primary source material and important background information about the world in which it was produced.

Each book in the series focuses on a specific topic within a specific historical period. Each provides a basis for lively thought and discussion about several aspects of the topic and the historian's role. Each is short enough (and inexpensive enough) to be a reasonable one-week assignment in a college course. Whether as classroom or personal reading, each book in the series provides firsthand experience of the challenge—and fun—of discovering, recreating, and interpreting the past.

Lynn Hunt
David W. Blight
Bonnie G. Smith
Natalie Zemon Davis
Ernest R. May

Preface

The U.S. War with Mexico was a pivotal event in American history. Not only did it set a precedent for the acquisition of foreign territory through war, but it also proved to be one of the causes of the American Civil War. As an expansionist war, it enabled the United States to incorporate a "conquered" population, with land and citizenship rights guaranteed by treaty, into the Republic. The war was also significant because of the increasing centrality of race both in defining Mexicans as the enemy and in debates about annexing Mexican land. Labeling Mexicans as "nonwhite" ensured that Americans would view them as the enemy both during the war and after. This in turn set a pattern for how the United States would regard its "enemies" in future military clashes. In addition, with the Wilmot Proviso of 1846, the newly acquired territory of northern Mexico became the vehicle through which the U.S. Congress and the American public debated slavery and its expansion in the 1850s. Consequently, the war contributed greatly to the ongoing tensions between the North and South over slavery. The war's influence continues to be felt politically, socially, and culturally. This volume seeks to provide students with a complex and nuanced understanding of the conflict and its long-term impact on the United States.

This book comprises two sections. The first is an introductory essay that examines the war's multifaceted nature, with an emphasis on the conflict's racialized dimensions. This section traces the war's origins by examining developments in the United States and Mexico, focusing on the unequal relationship between the two countries in the areas of nation building, economics, and territorial expansion. It shows that in essence, the war was a clash between two nations that had developed quite differently, with one ultimately becoming more powerful than the other. Within this context, American westward expansion, and the subsequent removal of Indian nations to reservations in the West and their treatment as colonized "others," emerged

as a rehearsal for how the federal government would deal with ethnic
Mexicans after the war. The introduction then focuses on Americans'
movement into Texas, the establishment of the Lone Star Republic,
and the diplomatic tensions in the wake of the United States' annexation of Texas. Along with examining key military campaigns, the introduction discusses reactions to the war by both ordinary Americans
and elites, including the production of poems, songs, and novels, as
well as the vocal resistance of such prominent individuals as John C.
Calhoun, Lucretia Mott, and Henry David Thoreau. Similarly, the
introduction explores Mexican citizens' responses to their northern
invaders. The discussion then focuses on the Treaty of Guadalupe
Hidalgo, with special attention given to the implications of incorporating citizens of another nation into the United States and in effect rendering them foreigners in their native land. Finally, the introduction
ponders the ideological and territorial ramifications of the war for both
republics.

Because this book seeks to provide a balanced view of the war, the
fifty-three documents in part two feature firsthand accounts from both
American and Mexican perspectives. They include political writings
that laid the foundation for U.S. westward expansion and outlined the
boundaries of American citizenship. They also present Mexican views
of American expansion and explore the intricacies of the breakdown
in diplomatic relations between the United States and Mexico. Politicians' perspectives on the war; American soldiers' accounts of the
battles; and samples of the poems, songs, and novels that the conflict
engendered also are included. In addition, part two contains documents reflecting prominent Americans' opposition to the war, the
Treaty of Guadalupe Hidalgo, Mexican politicians' views of the accord,
and Senator John C. Calhoun's ideas regarding the incorporation of
Mexicans into the American Republic. These voices are juxtaposed
with those of the inhabitants of the annexed territory and their views
of the new American order in the Southwest.

To facilitate students' understanding of the war, each document is
introduced with a headnote that explains the author's position and the
significance of the document. A map not only shows key cities and
battle sites but also vividly demonstrates how the war reshaped physical boundaries and territorial control. Other tools, such as gloss notes
and a chronology of events, will help students move through the material and trace major milestones. A series of questions at the end will
guide students' analysis of the documents. The volume ends with a
bibliography outlining important historical accounts of the U.S. War
with Mexico.

As a final note, I have titled this book *The U.S. War with Mexico* rather than using the more traditional "Mexican War" or "Mexican American War" for several reasons. First, the preferred designation shifts the focus to a conflict between two nations, rather than keeping the focus on one nation acting against another or on a conflict between peoples instead of countries. Second, the term "Mexican War" implies that Mexico was the aggressor, which was not the case. Finally, the new name doesn't include the word *Mexican*, which since the war has taken on a pejorative, racialized meaning. Using the phrase "U.S. War with Mexico" promotes a concentration on nation building, expansion, and race as the key causes of this conflict.

ACKNOWLEDGMENTS

Writing a book is a solitary yet collective experience. This is my attempt to thank the many people who accompanied me on my journey to produce this book. First among them is my former colleague Sherry Smith, who read several drafts of the original book proposal and offered sage advice about writing a book on a war. The outside readers who read the manuscript offered invaluable suggestions. I thank Kathryn A. Abbott, formerly of Western Kentucky University and currently at Bedford/St. Martin's; Kevin Hatfield, University of Oregon; Alan McPherson, Howard University; Stephen J. Pitti, Yale University; Leonard Sadosky, Iowa State University; Edmund Wehrle, Eastern Illinois University; and one anonymous reader whose close reading of the manuscript and substantive comments made for a sharper and more focused book.

My developmental editor, Debra Michals, not only guided the manuscript's content but also worked her magic to ensure that the text became crisper, clearer, and more robust. Copy editor Barb Jatkola's hard work and attention to detail have enhanced every aspect of this book. The Bedford/St. Martin's staff believed in this project from the beginning, and history series director for development Jane Knetzger pressed (and prodded) me to continue with it. Laurel Damashek answered my queries quickly and efficiently in the most courteous and professional manner.

I also thank Lilia Rosas for research help at a crucial moment. The Huntington Library's resources and scholarly community facilitated the writing of this book, and its staff provided information and assistance. For all their help, I thank Peter Blodgett, Bill Frank, Juan Gómez, and Susie Krasnoo.

My friends have been extremely supportive and have provided refuge from a sometimes all-encompassing project. Among those who deserve special mention are Chuck Ambler, Barbara Berglund, Bill Deverell, Julie Figueroa, Laura Gómez, Ben Johnson, Linus Kafka, Christian Lastra, Shaun Lewis, Beth Marchant, Lisa Miller, Michelle Nickerson, Dominique Padurano, Caetano Pérez-Marchant, Rafael Pérez-Torres, Richard Pineda, Gloria Rodríguez, Vicki Ruiz, Endi Silva, Stacey Sowards, and Lissa Wadewitz. Ryan Stanford's deep and abiding friendship eased this project's completion.

Students in my U.S. survey classes and Chicano/Chicana history courses at the University of Texas at El Paso have been the testing ground for the ideas in this book, making Oscar Hammerstein's words, "By your pupils you'll be taught," ring true.

Without my family, I'm nothing. I thank them for all they do for me, especially my parents, Bertha González Chávez and Alberto Chávez, who not only fed and housed me during the summers I worked on this book but also lent me their much-needed vehicles, which allowed me to dart around Southern California to gather sources. My niece Marisela R. Chávez generously lent me her laptop computer one summer and constantly helped me with odds and ends.

Finally, I want to thank my former professor and mentor, Norris Hundley Jr. Although his finely sharpened pencil did not help bring order to this book's pages, the skills he taught me aided in its production. Dedicating this book to him is my humble attempt to thank him for all he has done for me.

Ernesto Chávez

Contents

APPENDIXES

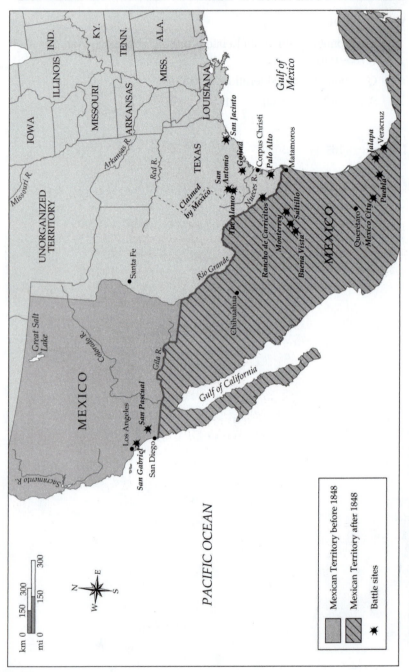

Contested Terrain in the U.S. War with Mexico

PART ONE

Introduction:
Race, Manifest Destiny,
and the U.S. War
with Mexico

Just before six on the evening of May 20, 1846, a band struck up "Come Sing Me That Simple Air Again," signaling the beginning of a mass gathering organized by New York City officials to support Congress's recent declaration of war against Mexico. The estimated twenty thousand people assembled in front of City Hall heard prominent citizens express enthusiasm for the war and castigate "the poor creatures" of Mexico. As the mayor adjourned the meeting, the crowd chanted "Dixon! Dixon!" and George Washington Dixon took the stage. An early blackface performer, Dixon addressed the people, saying, "I am going to defend our soil! I am going to march onward and plant our standard of liberty in the halls of the Montezuma!" Then, at the urging of the crowd, he sang:

> The Mexicans are on our soil,
> In war they wish us to embroil;
> They've tried their best and worst to vex us,
> By murdering our brave men in Texas.
> > *Chorus*—We're on our way to Rio Grande,
> > On our way to Rio Grande,
> > On our way to Rio Grande,
> > And with arms they'll find us handy.

> We are the boys who fear no noise,
> We'll leave behind us all our joys
> To punish those half-savage scamps,
> Who've slain our brethren in their camps. . . .
>
> The God of War, the mighty Mars,
> Has smiled upon our stripes and stars;
> And spite of any ugly rumors
> We'll vanquish all the Montezumas![1]

Dixon's lyrics outlined the war's causes. First, many racist notions would be used to justify the war. That Dixon was a blackface performer—a white man (although his enemies accused him of being "mulatto," or biracial) who pretended to be black, thus promulgating racism while providing entertainment—reveals the era's racist beliefs. His performance is ironic because most African Americans opposed the war, viewing it as a vehicle for spreading slavery. Dixon, then, exemplified proslavery advocates who presumed the right to speak for blacks. Racism also shaped the depiction of Mexicans as "half-savage scamps" and "Montezumas" in the song. Second, the lines "The God of War, the mighty Mars, / Has smiled upon our stripes and stars" reveal the centrality of nationalism and nation building to the conflict. Finally, the tune clearly shows that acquiring more land was a major motivation for the United States in pursuing the war. When Dixon says, "The Mexicans are on our soil," he is describing a contested portion of Texas as U.S. land, even though it was considered part of Mexico. Dixon's song encapsulates the main goal of this book: to examine the forces leading to the war, the conflict itself, and its aftermath, paying close attention to race and racialization, nationalism and nation building, and the U.S. quest for western territory.

MANIFEST DESTINY

In the 1840s, U.S. pursuit of western territory was inspired by the idea of manifest destiny, the belief that Americans had a God-given right, based on racial superiority, to expand to the Pacific Ocean. While the concept dated back to the Puritans, John L. O'Sullivan coined the phrase in 1845, first using it in his newspaper, the *United States Democratic Review* (Document 1). Soon manifest destiny became a staple of American political rhetoric. At its core, manifest destiny called for the territorial expansion of the United States and was a justification used by southerners for extending slavery. Thus, manifest destiny instilled nation building through territorial expansion, promoted the notion of American racial superiority, cast all nonwhites—Indians, Mexicans, and blacks—as inferior beings, and ultimately endorsed slavery's growth. (See the map on page xvi.)

NEIGHBORING REPUBLICS

The different ways the United States and Mexico had developed and become nations played a significant role in the war. Following the American Revolution, the former British colonies formed a federal republic based first on the Articles of Confederation and then on the U.S. Constitution in 1787. The Constitution granted full citizenship only to white, property-owning men. It also upheld slavery, establishing that, for the purpose of determining representation in the House of Representatives, five slaves equalled three white men.

In addition to the Constitution's citizenship restrictions, the new nation also established other racial limitations. Perhaps most telling was the Naturalization Act of 1790, which permitted only white persons to become naturalized U.S. citizens, thereby institutionalizing a racial prerequisite for citizenship (Document 2). The same year, Congress passed the Trade and Intercourse Act, which classified Indians as "foreign nations." Both acts show the Republic's concern with race politically and economically. Similarly, women were excluded from full citizenship. Although white women were granted some considerations—unmarried white women and widows could own land, for example—no woman could vote or hold office. Thus, the United States, which promised equality for all, in reality discriminated against blacks, Indians, and women.

Mexico's road to independence and the establishment of a federal republic looked much different. As proclaimed in 1810, the Mexican nation was a multiracial entity that guaranteed the rights of Indians, mestizos (people of mixed Indian and Spanish ancestry), *peninsulars* (those born in Spain), and Creoles (people of "pure" Spanish ancestry born in the Americas). When the wars of independence ended in 1821, Agustín de Iturbide, a Creole who had led the Mexican army against Spain, issued the Plan de Iguala to establish order and create a coalition of the various institutions and social groups in Mexico (Document 3). Iturbide soon established a Mexican empire and proclaimed himself its ruler, Agustín I.

In 1823, two years after its founding, the Mexican empire failed, and Iturbide was forced to abdicate. A year later, the Mexican Constitution

established the United States of Mexico as a federal republic comprising nineteen states and four territories (Document 4). A fundamental
difference between the United States and Mexico was that the Mexican republic included Indians as citizens. Although similar to the U.S.
Constitution, the Mexican Constitution adopted a broader definition of
citizenship, struggled directly with issues of social equality along
racial and gender lines, addressed the institution of hereditary chattel
slavery, and established few, if any, racial or property limitations on
the right to hold public office.

INDIANS AND WESTWARD EXPANSION

The United States believed that in order for the Republic to grow, it
needed to acquire western land. However, the West was inhabited by
various Indian tribes and claimed by other nations, particularly Spain,
France, and Mexico. Beginning in 1787 with the Northwest Ordinance, the United States established a procedure for inhabiting, and
ultimately incorporating, western land. As mentioned previously, the
Trade and Intercourse Act of 1790 designated Indian tribes as foreign
nations, so the United States could acquire Indian land only through
treaties negotiated by the federal government. Beginning in 1830,
however, with the passage of the Indian Removal Act (Document 5)
Indian tribes lost the power to retain their homelands. In 1831, the
Supreme Court ruled in *Cherokee v. Georgia* that Indian tribes were
not foreign nations but "domestic dependent nations." Consequently,
by the end of the 1830s, the United States was able to forcibly move
the Cherokee, Choctaw, Chickasaw, Seminole, and Creek nations from
the Southeast into Indian Territory (present-day Oklahoma). While the
United States robbed Indians of their sovereignty and subjugated
them as a people, the acquisition of their land facilitated nation building and ensured the ongoing pursuit of more territory. Indian removal, though a tragic and important event in its own right, is
significant in the context of the U.S. war with Mexico as a rehearsal
for how the United States would ultimately deal with the Mexicans.

The fledgling United States also negotiated treaties with European
powers. With the 1795 Treaty of San Lorenzo, the United States established diplomatic relations with Spain and set the border between
itself and Spain's North American possessions (Document 6). In 1803,
the United States purchased Louisiana from France for $15 million

(Document 7). As a result of this move, the United States not only doubled its size but also inherited the territory's Indian and European inhabitants. The status of Indian tribes had already been established, but the status of the French residents was another matter. The Louisiana Purchase Treaty accepted them as U.S. citizens, thus incorporating inhabitants of another country into the United States for the first time.

COLONIZING TEXAS

To understand what led to the conflict between the United States and Mexico in 1846, it is vital to explore how Texas was first colonized, America's role in this colonization, and the Texas War for Independence.

Until 1819, Spain barred American settlers from Texas for fear that the United States would try to annex the territory and claim it as part of the Louisiana Purchase. That year, however, the two countries signed the Adams-Onís Treaty, through which the United States purchased Florida and confirmed Spain's claim to Texas. Before long, a Missouri empresario named Moses Austin sought a royal commission to bring three hundred American families to Texas. Austin told the Spanish authorities that his settlement was interested only in growing sugarcane and cotton. Believing that the Americans could provide a buffer against Indians to the north, Spain granted Austin's petition in January 1821. Before anything could happen, Austin died and Mexico won its independence. Later that year, Moses's son Stephen approached the new Mexican government about settlement in Texas, and in December Mexico granted Stephen Austin a tract of rich land on the Brazos River, where he founded San Felipe de Austin. The only conditions of settlement were that Austin's group of three hundred had to be of good moral character, practice Catholicism, and abide by Mexican law.

Mexico granted these concessions as part of a larger nation-building strategy. By 1821, only 2,500 Mexican citizens had settled in Texas. This had much to do with the lack of silver mining in the region, which Mexico and many of its 6,000,000 residents relied on for their income. With its recent transformation to a republic, Mexico's notions of citizenship were fluid. In 1824, believing that the American settlers could be integrated into Mexican society, Mexico passed a colonization law that offered land and a seven-year tax exemption to

Americans who settled and developed the area (Document 8). While the United States looked to the West for expansion, Mexico looked to expand economic opportunities in its own territories and relied on American settlers to achieve that end.

A year later, the Coahuila-Texas State Colonization Law (Document 9) drew thousands of settlers, most of them Americans, to the state capital of Saltillo seeking land grants. By 1827, there were 12,000 U.S. citizens living in Texas and 5,000 Mexicans. Eight years later, there were 20,000 Americans, while the Mexican population remained unchanged. In addition, American Indians, particularly Cherokees, sought and obtained land in Texas. The colonization law did not allow entire Indian nations to petition for land, but rather offered individual Indians land in an attempt to break up tribes and assimilate individuals into Texas society. Because most Indians refused to convert to Catholicism, their prospects for obtaining land in Texas were limited.

Whereas Indians were straightforward about their inability to comply with all aspects of the colonization law, many Americans simply ignored its provisions. Most American immigrants never converted to Catholicism or bothered to learn Spanish. Simply put, transforming Americans into good Mexicans was virtually impossible, since their identity as Americans was already firmly established. In December 1826, this deeply entrenched American identity led some settlers near Nacogdoches, in eastern Texas, to attempt to secede from Mexico and establish an independent Republic of Fredonia. These rebels were quickly defeated, but the insurgency inspired U.S. popular and newspaper support for these so-called freedom fighters. This conflict and the U.S. response set the stage for accepting U.S. annexation of Texas years later.

American support for the Fredonia insurrection heightened Mexico's suspicion of U.S. designs. The presence of American minister Joel R. Poinsett in Mexico City also fostered mistrust of the United States. Poinsett was there to negotiate an accord that would allow the United States to negate the 1819 Adams-Onís Treaty and claim Texas as its own. Mexico prepared for the negotiations by searching its archives for all documents related to the boundary agreement and by establishing a commission in 1828 to survey the 1819 unmarked boundary.

The commission, under General Manuel Mier y Terán, also was charged with reporting on conditions in Texas. The investigation convinced the general that American immigration to Texas was the greatest single threat to Mexican security. Texas, he believed, was a vital part of the Mexican nation because its rich land could be used for agriculture and livestock, which would ensure Mexico's economic independence. As a result, Mier y Terán's 1829 report to the Mexican war minister suggested several measures to secure Texas, most importantly preventing the United States from expanding its influence there (Document 10).

The Mexican Congress responded with a law in the spring of 1830 that created a military occupation of Texas, encouraged colonization by Mexicans and Europeans, initiated stronger economic ties between Texas and the rest of Mexico, and made it illegal for Americans to enter the territory. Although American immigration to Texas continued, albeit illegally, this law, coupled with Mexican president Vicente Guerrero's September 1829 edict banning slavery in Mexico, caused Texans, especially American immigrants, to fear for their future. In December, after influential Texans convinced the Mexican government that banning slavery would have a detrimental effect on Texas, Guerrero exempted the province from the emancipation decree.

Texans, both American- and Mexican-born, also were unhappy about their unequal representation in the Coahuila-Texas legislature. Texas had three representatives, while Coahuila had nine, which meant that Texas was always at a disadvantage when voting on legislation. Another grievance was that all the appellate courts were located in Saltillo, in the southern part of the state, making most appeals too time-consuming and costly for Texans to pursue. Even so, a Mexican-ruled Texas seemed like a good place for free African Americans to live. American abolitionist Benjamin Lundy traveled to the region in 1833 to investigate the possibility of establishing a colony for free blacks there (Document 11).

TEXAS'S WAR FOR INDEPENDENCE

Antonio López de Santa Anna's rise to power in Mexico led to big changes in Texas. An enigmatic figure in Mexican history, Santa Anna viewed himself as the Napoleon of the West, complete with aristocratic pretensions. In truth, he was an opportunist whose charisma and military skills catapulted him to power. Initially attaining prominence during the War for Independence, Santa Anna continued his climb up the ladder of Mexican politics in 1829 when troops under his command defeated those sent by the Spanish king Ferdinand VII to reconquer Mexico. Despite his heroic status, he was not offered a position in President Guerrero's cabinet, and he retired to his hacienda in Veracruz.

In 1832, Santa Anna returned to the national spotlight when he was elected president. In January 1833, before his inauguration, he decided not to take office but to allow his vice president, Valentín Gómez Farías, to rule in his place. In May 1834, fearing that the nation was drifting toward civil war, Santa Anna replaced Gómez Farías as president. Though a longtime federalist who embraced the sovereignty of the states, Santa Anna now bowed to pressure from conservative politicians, the clergy, and the military to support a strong central government. Ruling by decree, he dissolved Congress and revoked the 1824 constitution, rescinded Gómez Farías's anticlerical laws, and canceled other liberal legislation.

Santa Anna embraced centralism and abandoned federalism because he feared that federalism would lead some Mexican states, including Texas, to secede. In reality, the opposite was true: The move toward centralism sparked widespread revolt throughout Mexico. The Mexican states of Zacatecas, Jalisco, San Luis Potosí, and Guanajuato formed a coalition to defend their sovereignty. The alliance was short-lived, and only Zacatecas assembled an army, which Santa Anna's troops ruthlessly defeated in May 1835. With the threat to his power obliterated, Santa Anna held elections for a new Congress composed only of conservatives, including those who embraced centralism and supported military power and the Catholic Church. By October 1835, this Congress had established a new centralist state in Mexico, which dissolved the state legislatures and transformed the former states into military departments governed by presidential appointees.

The actions of the Mexican government led Texans to engage in a war of secession. Fighting began on September 30, 1835, in Gonzales and moved to San Antonio. Meanwhile, on November 3, the Texan Consultation of Representatives met in San Felipe de Austin and established a provisional government for a proposed state of Texas within the Mexican republic. On December 5, 1835, after a stalemate of more than a month, fighting commenced in San Antonio when the Texans attacked a poorly trained army under the Mexican commander Martín Perfecto de Cos. Four days later, the Mexicans surrendered and marched south. The Texans, having taken San Antonio, moved into an abandoned mission known as the Alamo to reorganize.

The Mexican army under Santa Anna reached San Antonio on February 23, 1836. As the army planned its next move, the Texan Consultation of Representatives met in the town of Washington-on-the-Brazos on March 2 and adopted the Texas Declaration of Independence (Document 12). Instead of a Mexican state, however, the convention created a provisional government for an independent republic. It elected David Burnet as provisional president and Lorenzo de Zavala (a former Mexican diplomat who had participated in the 1824 Mexican constitutional convention and had fled Mexico when Santa Anna assumed power) as provisional vice president. The convention also confirmed Samuel Houston as commander in chief of the army.

Meanwhile, Santa Anna issued a decree declaring the Texans rebels who were acting against the interests of Mexico (Document 13). Furthermore, he recognized that the key to holding San Antonio was capturing the Alamo. About 150 men (including David Crockett, James Bowie, and William Barret Travis) and 2 women had taken refuge there and were prepared to defend the weak fort. On the morning of March 6, Santa Anna ordered 1,500 of his men to attack the garrison. The battle lasted about an hour. Eulalia Yorba, who witnessed the assault, recalled that the fighting had stopped by 6:30 A.M. (Document 14). The Mexicans outnumbered their enemy 10 to 1 and thus were able to claim victory. While the "Alamo martyrs" hold a lasting place in Texas history, their numbers pale in comparison to the 342 prisoners of war accused of piracy and executed at Goliad under Santa Anna's orders.

Though victorious at the Alamo, Santa Anna's troops were defeated by an army led by Sam Houston at the San Jacinto River on April 21. The Treaty of Velasco ended the hostilities. In exchange for his safe return to Mexico, Santa Anna agreed to recognize Texas's independence and to withdraw Mexican troops to positions south of the Rio Grande. He also secretly agreed to form a commission that would officially recognize Texas's independence, but once he returned to Mexico, he abandoned the plan. Since the treaty was signed while Santa Anna was a prisoner of war, the Mexican Congress repudiated it and promised to continue fighting for the territory. Following the war, the independent Texans created a republic that protected slavery and subjugated blacks, Indians, and, eventually, Mexicans. The 1840 census of the Texas republic shows that there were 35,000 Texans of American descent, 4,000 Mexicans, and 12,000 African American slaves. Although there is no official number for Indians, who were considered outside the political community, one historian has estimated that there

were 40,000 Indians in Texas at the time. Texans also voted to petition
the United States for statehood.

THE REPUBLIC OF TEXAS AND
U.S.-MEXICO DIPLOMATIC RELATIONS

Americans watched the Texas revolution closely and interpreted it as
a revolt against an unjust government and, more important, a racial
clash. Newspapers in the United States publicized the battles and ven-
omously condemned the Mexican people. The fact that Mexicans
were a mixed people, the product of the miscegenation of Spaniards
and Indians, caused Americans to denigrate them as worthless. Thus,
Mexicans entered the script of racial America. These notions would be
played out in the war between the United States and Mexico—a conflict that would have Texas at its center.

Different interpretations of Texas's status heightened tensions
between the United States and Mexico. Whereas Mexico viewed
Texas as a province in revolt, the United States recognized it as an
independent republic on March 3, 1837. This, and the participation of
U.S. citizens in the struggle for Texas's independence, damaged diplomatic relations between the two nations. Mexican political rhetoric
constantly raised the possibility of sending a military expedition to
punish Texas, but the country's shaky political situation and lack of
economic resources made invasion impossible. Although Mexico
could not reclaim Texas, public opinion prevented the Mexican government from recognizing its independence. In light of the United
States' support of Texas, one Mexico City newspaper, *El Mosquito
Mexicano*, castigated the United States as Mexico's true enemy and
called for a renewal of war not against Texas, but against "the entire
Northern nation" (Document 15).

General Anastasio Bustamante, a candidate in Mexico's 1837 presidential election, declared that should he win, he would recover Texas.
Once he took office, however, he was unable to mobilize the nation and
realized that such an attempt would lead to war with the United States
By October 1838, antigovernment uprisings had emerged throughout
the country. Conditions worsened when impoverished Mexico failed
to repay a loan it had received from France and faced the threat of an
invasion by that country. With the nation's coffers empty, discontent
among the masses spread.

Whatever Mexicans felt about the United States, the Latin American nation could not attack its northern neighbor. Mexico remained destabilized by fighting between the federalists and the centralists. Although it might have had the resources to wage war, the federalists would not support the national army, while the centralists would not appropriate church land or tax the rich to raise revenues to fund the fight.

How to deal with Texas was a volatile issue in the United States as well. The admission of Texas to the Union would tilt the balance of slave and free states. Under the 1820 Missouri Compromise, Texas would become a slave state because of its location below latitude 36°30'. U.S. leaders also recognized that annexation could cause a war with Mexico. Although President Andrew Jackson supported the annexation of Texas, the growing abolitionist movement and his lame-duck status in 1836 prevented him from acting. Martin Van Buren, Jackson's successor in 1837, was constrained by the economic depression of 1837.

The situation between the two countries worsened when U.S. citizens began making claims against the Mexican government for losses they had incurred while doing business in Mexico. Because of Mexico's unstable political situation, a disorderly social atmosphere was prevalent and the frequent revolts and revolutions ensured that even in the major urban centers life and property were not safe. Both foreigners and Mexicans suffered alike. However, American citizens living and doing business in Mexico claimed that the Mexican government was responsible for these injuries and financial losses and demanded recompense. The U.S. government supported these claims, which dated back to 1826, and demanded payment. In 1839, the nations agreed to let an international tribunal resolve the matter. U.S. citizens were awarded $2 million of the $9 million they sought. Mexico made installment payments with money acquired through forced loans[2] until 1844, when relations between the countries broke down. The U.S. government's persistent support of its citizens' claims against its impoverished neighbor further tarnished its image in Mexico. By 1840, Mexico had a deficit of 14 million pesos, resulting mostly from the Texas revolution, the French threat of invasion, and the need to maintain an army along the northern frontier.

While Mexico's dire financial situation continued, it sustained further territorial threats from land-hungry Americans. The first incident occurred in the summer of 1842, when the Texas–Santa Fe expedition[3] invaded the Mexican state of New Mexico. The New Mexicans soon defeated the invaders, but that fall, acting on a rumor of an imminent war between the United States and Mexico, U.S. Pacific Fleet commander Lieutenant Thomas ap Catesby Jones seized the Mexican fortress in Monterey, California. Learning of his mistake, he apologized and was relieved of his command. By 1843, Mexico believed that the United States had designs on more of its territory.

In the midst of this conflict, Texas reemerged as a source of tension between Mexico and the United States. Despite U.S. reluctance to admit Texas to the Union, when Great Britain and France arranged a truce between Mexico and Texas in 1843, U.S. fears of European influence on the new republic led to renewed calls for annexation. Some Americans also supported annexation because they were afraid that Texas's geographic location would give it an advantage in acquiring territory in the Southwest, particularly California and the Pacific coast. If Texas became a state rather than remaining an independent republic, any territorial ambitions it had would be eliminated. The prospect of annexation was, of course, met with hostility in Mexico. Back in power, Antonio López de Santa Anna, perhaps presuming that he would have European support, echoed General Bustamante's declaration that annexation would cause war.

In early 1844, a resolution on the annexation of Texas was brought before the U.S. Senate. The measure failed to get the required two-thirds majority. The issue would prove instrumental in the 1844 presidential election, however, when the Democrats nominated James K. Polk, a relatively unknown Tennessean, over former president Martin Van Buren. Polk ran on the promise of "reannexation," claiming that Texas rightfully belonged to the United States under the Louisiana Purchase but had been given to Spain in 1819 through the "blunder" of the Adams-Onís Treaty. His other promise was the "reoccupation" of Oregon, which had been held jointly by the United States and Great Britain since 1818. Whig Party candidate Henry Clay opposed Texas statehood, and when he lost by a narrow margin, expansionists touted Polk's victory as a mandate for annexation. Perhaps wanting to steal Polk's thunder, lame-duck president John Tyler almost immediately called for a joint congressional resolution for annexation, which required approval by a simple majority rather than a two-thirds vote. The resolution passed in February 1845. The Texan Convention of Representatives approved the annexation resolution in June, the people of Texas ratified it in October, and the new state entered the Union in December, despite Massachusetts senator Daniel Webster's speech conveying his concerns about annexation (Document 16).

By that time, Santa Anna had been overthrown in a revolution that brought President José Herrera to power. Herrera was obligated to respond to Texas's annexation, but with an empty treasury, an army in shambles, and no European support, he had few options. In the spring of 1845, he tried unsuccessfully to prevent annexation by agreeing to recognize Texas's independence if it refused to join the United States. Meanwhile, Polk sent John Slidell, whom he dubbed "envoy extraordinaire and minister plenipotentiary," to Mexico to negotiate the Texas border dispute. However, Herrera refused to receive Slidell with his designated title given that following the U.S. annexation of Texas diplomatic relations between the two nations had ceased to exist. Although Herrera had agreed to discuss the matter of the Texas boundary and the American claims with a U.S. commissioner, he had not agreed to do so with a diplomat bearing the title of minister—which designated that diplomatic relations existed—let alone one with the rank of "envoy extraordinaire and minister plenipotentiary." Mexico believed that the only way that full diplomatic relations could occur was if it received compensation for the loss of Texas. However, Herrera acted slowly in dismissing Slidell, which made him appear weak in the eyes of his enemies and perhaps willing to agree to give in to U.S. demands. Thus, when he ordered General Mariano Paredes y Arrillaga to move his troops from San Luis Potosí to the Mexican-U.S. border, Paredes marched on Mexico City and deposed him. With Paredes in power, many Mexicans believed that the nation's honor and its future were saved. But like Herrera, Paredes seemed to do nothing, sparking criticism and hostility from former supporters.

TOWARD WAR

Meanwhile, the United States took the first steps toward war. In June 1845, Polk instructed General Zachary Taylor to move his army to Corpus Christi, Texas, and approach the Rio Grande. Polk also ordered naval forces to the Gulf of Mexico and requested the strengthening of the Pacific coast. He again dispatched Slidell to Mexico to purchase California for $25 million and New Mexico for $5 million and to settle the Texas border at the Rio Grande rather than the Nueces River. Polk believed that debt-ridden Mexico would gladly sell these territories to raise funds, but the Mexican government was insulted by the offer.

The Texas border dispute proved a sensitive issue. Since the republic's founding, Texans had claimed that the Rio Grande formed the border with Mexico. With annexation, the United States upheld that claim, despite countless Spanish and Mexican maps placing the boundary farther north, at the Nueces River. Texans further asserted that the border began at the Rio Grande's point of origin in present-day southern Colorado. Setting the border at the Rio Grande would tie Texas to both trade on the Santa Fe Trail, which lay at the river's source, and commercial dealings at Matamoros, whose harbor was located at the waterway's end. Consequently, the Lone Star Republic claimed not only that San Antonio and Laredo were part of Texas but also that Albuquerque and the rest of present-day New Mexico were within its limits. This pronouncement seriously encroached on Mexican land. In January 1846, Slidell was expelled from Mexico, with Mexico arguing that it had agreed only to discuss American claims, not negotiate the sale of territory. Even before Slidell's expulsion, in October 1845 Polk ordered Taylor to move his troops south of the Nueces River. The United States also stationed troops along the California coast and in New Mexico.

When President Paredes became aware of the American advance to the Rio Grande, he dispatched Commander Pedro de Ampudia to Matamoros. On April 12, 1846, Ampudia told Taylor to retreat immediately to the north side of the Nueces River. Refusing to leave, Taylor replied that Ampudia would be responsible for any hostilities that might commence (Document 18). Taylor ordered the U.S. Navy to blockade the mouth of the Rio Grande, cutting off supplies to the Mexican troops in Matamoros. On April 23, Paredes declared the initiation of a defensive war against the United States and sent General Mariano Arista, commander of the Army of the North, to Matamoros to attack U.S. troops. On April 25, the Mexican army attacked a squadron of American dragoons at Rancho de Carricitos, located between the Nueces River and the Rio Grande. The next day, Taylor sent a dispatch to the adjutant general of the army informing him that eleven dragoons had been killed, five had been wounded, and forty-seven had been taken prisoner (Document 19).

News of the skirmish reached Washington on May 9. Two days later, Polk asked Congress for a declaration of war against Mexico (Document 20). Not everyone in Congress wanted to grant his request. Most of the opposition came from Whig Party members, but some Democrats also opposed it, most notably Senator John C. Calhoun of South Carolina. He and the Whigs denied that the Rio Grande marked the Texas border and argued that Polk had provoked the war by ordering Taylor to advance to the river. Only those Whigs belonging to the party's antislavery faction voted against the declaration of war, however, and the measure passed both houses of Congress by an overwhelming majority on May 13.

The declaration of war against Mexico turned Polk's attention to the nation's northern border, too. Remember that Polk had promised the "reoccupation" of Oregon, which had been occupied jointly by the United States and Great Britain since 1818. A treaty in 1842 had settled the U.S.-Canadian border west to Oregon, but with a large number of U.S. citizens moving into the Northwest, the Democratic Party was now calling for the annexation of Oregon. War with Mexico made Polk eager to settle the Oregon question, and in June 1846 he agreed to split the territory at the forty-ninth parallel. In doing so, Polk gave up what many expansionists believed was merely a barren stretch of land that would eventually belong to the United States anyway.

Because of its racialized outlook, America dealt with Great Britain differently than it did with Mexico. Whereas the Mexicans were viewed as inferior, half-breed products of racial mixing, the English were seen as purebred equals who possessed many commonalities with Americans. Thus, while the United States was waging war against Mexico over territory, it was negotiating a peaceful settlement with Great Britain. Once the Oregon issue was resolved, Polk could concentrate on the Mexican conflict.

Polk continued to face opposition to the war from Whigs in Congress, who believed that it would lead to the expansion of slavery. Whig criticism of the president intensified on August 8, 1846, when Polk asked Congress for $2 million—to be used at his discretion—to ease tensions between the two nations. In reality, Polk wanted this "Two-Million-Dollar Bill" to pay Mexico for California, New Mexico, and other territories. Although the Whig response varied, most demanded revisions ensuring that the president would not use the money to buy more land but solely to settle the border dispute that had caused the war. They feared that any Mexican land acquired by the United States would become slave territory under the Missouri Compromise. Representative Hugh White of New York announced that he would vote for the bill only if it were amended to prevent slavery from being established in any territory acquired from Mexico (Document 21).

Democratic Party member David Wilmot, a congressman from Pennsylvania, met White's challenge by authoring a proviso to the bill. It stated that the acquisition of any Mexican territory could occur only if slavery or other involuntary servitude were prohibited (Document 22). Wilmot was expressing northern Democrats' dissatisfaction with the Polk administration and their desire to appeal to the party's burgeoning antislavery constituency. The proviso altered the character of the proceedings on the bill, as members of Congress regrouped along sectional rather than party lines. Although the bill with the attached proviso passed in the House of Representatives, Democrats in the Senate prevented it from reaching a vote, thereby denying Polk the funds. From that point on, whenever antislavery wording was attached to an appropriation bill brought before Congress, the wording would effectively kill the measure, as the nation continued to divide along sectional lines.

Despite its defeat, the Wilmot Proviso changed the course of the debate by linking the issue of slavery with the war. President Polk failed to see the connection, but when Congress reconvened in December, the issues of war and slavery were inseparable. That the war was being fought to extend slavery was not lost on Frederick Douglass. Perhaps the most famous African American in the United States and beyond, Douglass opposed the war on the premise that slavery would be allowed in any land acquired from Mexico, just as it had been in Texas (Document 23).

POPULAR OPINION AND THE WAR IN THE UNITED STATES

The conflict with Mexico captured the attention and imagination of the general public, due in large part to America's racial mind-set. Americans "exoticized" Mexico, a distant land with a tropical climate and an alien (albeit inferior) people who spoke a foreign language. Hungry for information and updates, the populace turned to newspapers, and editors from New Orleans to New York sent reporters to Mexico. Their dispatches intensified the public's interest and ultimately ensured widespread support for the war.

One example of the war's popularity was the mass rally on May 20, 1846, in New York City described earlier. The night's speeches painted Mexicans as half-breed villains and called for the invasion of their land. Newspapers similarly backed the war; the most noteworthy was the *New York Herald* (Document 24). Walt Whitman shared these sentiments in his editorials for the *Brooklyn Daily Eagle*, writing that "Mexico must be thoroughly chastized" (Document 25).

While the war proved popular in most of the country, support lagged in the Northeast. New England was the hotbed of opposition for several reasons. First, located far from the battle itself, it was not endangered by fighting in the Southwest. Second, the region was the center of abolitionism and thus unsympathetic to what was perceived as a southern slaveholders' war for the expansion of slavery. Perhaps the most famous clergyman to speak against the war was New England Congregational minister and noted transcendentalist Theodore Parker, who denounced the conflict in "A Sermon of the Mexican War" at an antiwar meeting in Boston in June 1846 (Document 26). Unlike other critics, Parker's friend Henry David Thoreau took an individualistic approach to dissent, which he outlined in his essay "On Civil Disobedience" (Document 27).

Clergymen and reformers outside New England also opposed the war. Abolitionists in Ohio, western New York, and Pennsylvania assailed the war, along with Unitarians and Quakers nationwide. Women formed a large contingent of antiwar protesters. The women of Philadelphia were helped along in their peace efforts by American reformer Elihu Burritt, who asked the women of Exeter, England, to write a letter to the women of Philadelphia in which they would pledge their commitment to peace between their two countries. The American women responded to the letter by writing their own statement of peace, which was read at a public meeting on June 17, 1846, where abolitionist and later women's rights advocate Lucretia Mott read the address (Document 28). Women attended antiwar meetings in Ohio as well and wrote antiwar tracts.

Typically middle-class white women, these antiwar advocates extended the tenets of what historians have termed the "cult of domesticity" beyond women's role within the home to include a kind of social housekeeping. Earlier, beginning in the 1820s, women likewise broadened their social role by joining volunteer organizations that embraced the cause of the downtrodden. Some women reformers eventually joined the abolitionist movement, and when confronted with gender inequality that seemed to parallel racial inequality, several emerged as women's rights advocates. Opposition to the war clearly transformed these women. In advocating for peace, they entered a male domain and began to challenge the barriers that kept them from full citizenship.

The cult of domesticity also helped middle-class white women and men distinguish themselves from those whom they regarded as inferior. This outlook is clearly present in Susan Shelby Magoffin's diary entries. Accompanying her merchant husband, Samuel, down the Santa Fe Trail, Magoffin encountered Mexican men and women, and her observations clearly show that racialized notions of whiteness prevented her from appreciating Mexican women's differences (Document 29). Male observers offered another perspective, arguing that U.S. soldiers could marry Mexican women and regenerate the Mexican race. These views complemented theories of Anglo-Saxon superiority and brought another dimension to the war in Mexico. Marriage to Mexican women would peacefully incorporate both women and land. These sexual unions also would cleanse Mexico of "inferior" racial traits and ultimately return it to its "pure" Caucasian roots. Soldiers engaged in the war applied these ideas in their descriptions of Mexican women. While Mexican men were depicted as weak and inferior, Mexican women were portrayed as virtuous, brave, and pious, with the potential to create a new race if paired with the appropriate partners (Document 30).

Literature and the popular arts similarly reflected a racialized mindset. Like the writings that existed before the war, the literature emerging from the conflict exoticized Mexico and Mexicans. In these stories, an American hero typically encountered a group of Mexicans in need of assistance, which he, of course, provided. A good example is Henry William Herbert's 1848 novel *Pierre the Partisan: A Tale of the Mexican Marches*, which relates an American adventurer's encounter with a unit of U.S. dragoons as he guides them away from danger (Document 31).

The war also inspired popular songs, collected and published in pocket-size editions. Philadelphian William M'Carty compiled one of the most popular volumes, titled *National Songs, Ballads, and Other Patriotic Poetry Chiefly Relating to the War of 1846.* It included "Song of the Volunteers," sung to the minstrel melody of "Old Dan Tucker," which George Washington Dixon performed at the New York City rally in May 1846 (Document 32).

Poetry also proved popular during the war. Mexican war poets were, for the most part, unknown, and their identities have been lost. However, two famous American writers, John Greenleaf Whittier and James Russell Lowell, wrote verses to protest the conflict in Mexico. Whittier wrote three poems with war themes. His most enduring one, "The Angels of Buena Vista," was based on a report that several Mexican women stayed near the battlefield to aid their wounded soldiers (Document 33). Lowell's collection of protest poems, *The Biglow Papers*, also was popular. Written in a New England dialect and attributed to the fictional Hosea Biglow, the poems expressed Lowell's belief that the war was about extending slavery and would turn northerners into white slaves (Document 34).

WAGING THE WAR

On May 14, 1846, President Polk, together with Secretary of War William L. Marcy and General Winfield Scott, hurriedly crafted a master war plan with a three-pronged offensive. First, Taylor would remain on the Rio Grande and then push into northern Mexico. Second, a large overland expedition would be dispatched from San Antonio to Chihuahua, and a smaller force would proceed from Missouri to Santa Fe. Finally, an army of occupation would travel to Mexico City, and early on the U.S. Navy would barricade the Mexican ports of Tampico and Veracruz in the Gulf of Mexico.

After the incident at Rancho de Carricitos, Taylor's strategy was to take hold of the area north of the Rio Grande and then cross the river into Mexico. His aim in the north was to control Monterrey, crucial because its capture would secure northern Mexico and the Rio Grande area. Although Taylor believed that his army of six thousand men could easily take Monterrey, the Mexican government fortified the city with more than seven thousand troops. The city's natural setting, with rugged Independence Hill overlooking it to the west and the Santa Catalina River to the south and the east, made Monterrey difficult to penetrate. Taylor decided to attack the city from the north. He also bombarded the town and prevented reinforcements from entering. A woman known as Dos Amades, commanding a company of lancers, was among those leading the charge against the "Northern Barbarians." She "unsexed herself," according to one American officer, by dressing in a captain's uniform and leading a devastating charge (Document 35). Still, she could not defeat the American force. On September 25, Taylor captured Monterrey and moved to take the rest of northern Mexico, conquering Saltillo on November 16. By the end of 1846, northeastern Mexico was in American hands.

Believing that taking the rest of northern Mexico would end the war sooner, Taylor moved south in early February 1847. The mission proved bloody when Mexican horsemen attacked the American army near the village of Buena Vista on February 22. Warned of their approach, American volunteers and dragoons were waiting for them. Although the Americans were victorious, the Battle of Buena Vista was the war's costliest contest to date, lasting a day and a half. On the U.S. side, 665 were killed, while the Mexican dead numbered 3,500. In Samuel Chamberlain's account of the war, *My Confession*, he described the end of the battle as especially bloody (Document 36). Journalist Ramón Alcaraz recalled that the Mexican army suffered deeply during the battle (Document 37). Buena Vista ended the campaign in northern Mexico and changed the U.S. strategy in the region from offensive to purely defensive.

As Taylor and his army were fighting south of the Rio Grande, other American forces advanced into Mexico's far northern frontier in the present-day U.S. Southwest and California. To protect the significant trade route to Santa Fe, Colonel Stephen Watts Kearny led an army into New Mexico. Sensing a lack of support from the Mexican army, Governor Manuel Armijo disbanded his troops on August 16 and left for Chihuahua before the Americans arrived in Santa Fe (Document 38). Without an army, the New Mexicans could do little to prevent Kearny from marching into the capital on August 18. Within five weeks of his arrival, Kearny moved on to California to help a small band of U.S. citizens there.

Though usually called a bloodless conquest, the U.S. takeover of New Mexico was far from it. Bored in overcrowded Santa Fe, American forces began attacking New Mexican civilians. In response, the New Mexicans planned a revolt, which would include the assassination of Governor Charles Bent. When their plot was uncovered in December 1846, the conspirators were arrested, leading American authorities to believe that peace had been secured. In January 1847, however, others took up the cause and killed Bent. The rebels, numbering more than three thousand, raided and burned stores owned by U.S. citizens, winning support throughout northern New Mexico. Eventually, the U.S. army quelled the insurrection. Fifteen rebels were tried for murder or treason and subsequently executed, thereby ensuring no further mass violence against the American occupation. Meanwhile, on December 12, 1846, Colonel Alexander Doniphan and his men began their march toward El Paso del Norte on the banks of the Rio Grande, en route to their final destination of Chihuahua, which they captured by month's end.

The conquest of California held a larger significance for the war and for the United States' territorial ambitions. In January 1846, months before fighting began on the Rio Grande, the U.S. government sent John C. Frémont and an army to California to explore the Pacific coast. There Frémont met with the American consul, Thomas O. Larkin, to plan seizing the territory for the United States. The Mexican government, remembering Thomas ap Catesby Jones's actions in Monterey in 1842, ordered Frémont and his men to leave. En route to the Oregon border, Frémont received a message from the U.S. government informing him of impending hostilities on the Rio Grande, and he reversed his course to assume an active role in the capture of California.

Remaining in the Sonoma area for most of June and July, Frémont and his men engaged in several skirmishes, arrested Mexican general Mariano G. Vallejo, and were instrumental in sparking the Bear Flag Revolt, which on July 4, 1846, declared the short-lived Bear Flag Republic. Once Frémont received word that fighting had begun between U.S. and Mexican troops in the Rio Grande area, he claimed California for the United States. He then moved his men to Monterey to join other American troops in the conquest of California. Meanwhile, on July 7, after learning about fighting at Palo Alto, Texas, and Resaca de la Palma, Texas, Commodore John Drake Sloat captured Monterey. Three days later, he occupied San Francisco. When Commodore Robert F. Stockton arrived in California in mid-July, Sloat was relieved of his command. Once Frémont reached Monterey on July 19, Stockton allowed him to lead the California Battalion, as the Bear Flaggers now called themselves.

In late July, Stockton dispatched Frémont and his men to San Diego to move against the Mexican stronghold of Los Angeles. On August 13, Stockton and his men occupied Los Angeles without opposition, with Stockton proclaiming himself governor of the territory. He then left for San Francisco, believing that things were secure in the south. In late September, however, Stockton received word that the Mexicans living in California, called Californios, had revolted and his Los Angeles garrison had surrendered after a week of fighting. Returning south and reaching San Pedro, the port of Los Angeles, in late October, with no sign of Frémont, Stockton moved on to San Diego in November. On December 6, Kearny and his men reached San Diego, California's southernmost city, and encountered the Mexican army at nearby San Pascual. The Americans were victorious in the ensuing battle, but the conflict proved bloody. Kearny was wounded, and a third of his men were killed.

With Kearny's men resting in San Diego, Stockton moved toward Los Angeles on December 29. His troops met with little opposition until they reached the city's outskirts. On January 8 they encountered a force of five hundred Californios at the San Gabriel River. Attacking the Californios, the Americans forced them to retreat. On January 10, 1847, as Stockton prepared to retake Los Angeles, a delegation of Angelenos (Los Angeles residents), doubtful that they could protect their city, sought a truce. Once the Mexican forces evacuated the city, the civilian population surrendered Los Angeles to Stockton for the second time. Two days later, Frémont arrived on the city's outskirts. On January 13, he negotiated the Treaty of Cahuenga, which guaranteed Californios the same rights as U.S. citizens. Thus, by early 1847, the territory was secured and the fighting was over, except for an occasional revolt.

With northern Mexico now under U.S. control, only the south remained to be captured. In October 1846, President Polk had decided to land troops in Veracruz and then send them to Mexico City along the same route Hernán Cortés had taken to the capital in 1519. This plan was undoubtedly inspired by W. H. Prescott's 1843 *History of the Conquest of Mexico*, a widely read book that was popular among officers and enlisted men. The book repeated the era's racist sentiments about Mexicans, portraying them as weak and effeminate and arguing that the Spanish and the Aztecs exhibited the extremes of conquest and barbarism. Prescott's book instilled American soldiers with the idea that the conquest of Mexico was part of the United States' manifest destiny.

Led by Major General Winfield Scott, the first wave of U.S. invasion forces landed on the beach below Veracruz on March 9, 1847. After a week of preparation, the city was sealed off from the rear, and by March 22 it was completely surrounded. When Veracruz refused to surrender, Scott ordered its bombardment. After four days of fire, negotiations began, and three days later, on March 29, U.S. forces marched into the city. From Veracruz, Scott and his men proceeded to Mexico City. Along the way, the Americans defeated the Mexican army at Cerro Gordo on April 18. Although Santa Anna tried to prevent the Americans from taking the city of Puebla, on May 15 four thousand U.S. troops moved into Puebla, and by month's end it had become General Scott's headquarters. With eighty thousand residents, Puebla was the largest urban center that Scott's men had ever seen. One of these men was Massachusetts native Ralph W. Kirkham, who wrote about the city in his journal (Document 39). Five hundred new U.S. troops landed in Mexico in early August and soon reached Puebla. Wasting no time, Scott moved his men toward Mexico City on August 7.

The American army split up and took two roads to Mexico City, encountering Mexican troops en route and emerging victorious in battles at Contreras and Churubusco. Following the loss at Churubusco, the Mexican army's future seemed hopeless. Scott offered a truce, but Santa Anna declined on September 6. Scott then began to plan his assault on the capital, commencing with Chapultepec Castle, a military academy located on a two-hundred-foot crest on the city's edge. With that taken, Scott reasoned, American troops could enter the capital through its western gates. In the early morning of September 13, U.S. forces began blasting the castle. The shelling continued for fourteen hours, as the 832 defenders, including cadets at the military college, stood their ground. Dead and wounded soldiers lined the castle's corridors, receiving no medical attention. Santa Anna knew that the castle was becoming a morgue, and he refused to send reinforcements. The next morning, 500 U.S. infantrymen attacked.

By sunrise, the U.S. flag was flying over the castle. Losing Chapultepec was a serious blow to the Mexican resistance. Nevertheless, as Scott's army moved toward the Gates of Belen and San Cosmé, Mexican soldiers defended the passageway to the city until they exhausted their ammunition. When the U.S. forces finally broke through, fighting spread into the streets of the capital, lasting until evening. Santa Anna still had 12,000 men in the city, versus Scott's 6,000, and the possibility remained that the Mexican army would continue to fight, assisted by civilians. However, civil authorities persuaded Santa Anna to withdraw and regroup. The Mexican leaders then surrendered their capital to the North American invaders and relocated the government to Querétaro, one hundred miles to the north. Convinced that he could not win the war and unwilling to accept responsibility for defeat, on September 16, 1847, Santa Anna resigned the presidency and soon left the country.

The U.S. conquerors marched into Mexico City the next morning. The possibility of warfare continued until a peace treaty was signed. Thus, when General John E. Wool took control of the city, he instituted martial law and transformed the U.S. force into an army of occupation.

Their role as conquerors did not prevent at least one military officer from being captivated by Mexico City. In a letter to his wife, General Gideon Johnson Pillow shared his fascination with the capital's beauty (Document 40). While the U.S. military occupied the city, merchants catered to them, providing fandangos (dances or parties), a gambling house, and saloons. From September 1847 to March 1848, American forces even published a bilingual newspaper, the *American Star*, which carried official army dispatches, news of daily life in Mexico City, and classified ads (Document 41). Yet according to one of the city's residents, the U.S. invasion of the capital was a horrific experience for Mexicans (Document 42).

In January 1848, U.S. and Mexican diplomats began forging a peace treaty. Before peace was declared, Congress began to debate the annexation of all of Mexico, a proposal referred to as the "All Mexico Movement." Race, territorial expansion, and nation building were the core issues in the Senate debates. Whigs joined Democrats such as John C. Calhoun in opposing the Polk administration's effort to take territory in the interior of Mexico. On January 4, Calhoun delivered a speech calling for a defensive line strategy[4] and outlining the dangers of annexing all of Mexico (Document 43). To Calhoun, annexing Mexico meant that an inferior people would be incorporated into the U.S. Republic. Both Whigs and Democrats reiterated and expanded upon Calhoun's argument.

The debates over the "All Mexico Movement" resurrected several issues that had been important since the Republic's founding. Among them were who should be included in the Republic, how large it should be, and whether its survival could be ensured in the face of fundamental differences among its inhabitants. These concerns would, of course, be revisited in the decade preceding the Civil War. Thus, these debates would not only foreshadow the disputes of the 1850s but also, in many ways, cause them. They were cut short, however, when news arrived in mid-February that a peace treaty had been completed and delivered to the president for consideration.

THE TREATY OF GUADALUPE HIDALGO

From the beginning of the war, both the United States and Mexico sought a way to end what they mutually perceived as a potentially long and bloody conflict. After several unsuccessful attempts at forging a peace, in April 1847 Polk sent Undersecretary of State and Chief Clerk

Nicholas P. Trist to Mexico with a draft treaty. Secretary of State Buchanan told Trist that he had leeway in closing the accord, but that the Californias (upper and lower), New Mexico, and the Texas boundary were not negotiable. Because of the continued fighting and the reluctance of the Mexican government to appear weak, Trist did not make contact with Mexican authorities until June. Negotiations began on September 1, lasted five days, and then broke down because Polk would not compromise on the Rio Grande boundary and Santa Anna would cede only the area north of Monterey, California, to the United States. He would not part with any of New Mexico.

Mexican politicians published a lengthy letter arguing for continuing the war and stressing their reluctance to endorse any agreement that would cede national territory. Hearing about the letter, Polk decided that Trist should be recalled, since Mexico would negotiate only if the terms were different. Trist became the Mexican government's only hope for resolution, and thus he gained the upper hand in the negotiations. He held fast to the United States' territorial ambitions, refusing to yield on the Rio Grande boundary or on Mexican cession of New Mexico and California. Ultimately, he gave up only one U.S. stipulation: in return for San Diego, he dropped the demand to cross the Isthmus of Tehuantepec unencumbered.[5]

The Polk administration's handling of the treaty, which was signed on February 2, coupled with the Senate debate over ratification, clearly demonstrates that Mexico had become a subjugated nation. After the treaty reached Washington on February 19, 1848, Polk sent a message to Congress recommending two changes to the treaty: (1) the insertion of a secret article protecting its validity and (2) the elimination of Article X, which declared that the United States would respect land grants given by the Spanish and Mexican governments to residents of the ceded territories. This article was aimed specifically at protecting land grants in Texas, and Polk objected to it on the grounds that it would affect the property grants made by the Texas republic following its independence.

Although the president endorsed the treaty, the issues of territory and race, expressed in the debate over slavery's expansion, stalled ratification in the Senate. Ultimately, the Senate ratified the treaty only after making changes that would have lasting and significant effects on the Mexican population in the ceded territories. By striking Article X from the treaty, the Senate ensured that Mexican residents in the ceded territories would lose their land grants. In addition, the Senate changed the wording of Article IX by adding the citizenship guarantees of the Louisiana Purchase and Adams-Onís Treaty. This meant that U.S. citizenship was automatic for Mexicans; they could not choose to retain any previous citizenship status. But the article labeled them as a conquered people. By deeming Mexicans an in-between people who would be granted the rights of U.S. citizens but not always the ability to exercise them, Article IX allowed for the construction of a Mexican race in the United States. In addition, in 1848 U.S. citizenship was contingent on being a citizen of a state; the concept of federal citizenship would not emerge until 1868 with the Fourteenth Amendment. Thus, Mexican Americans would become full-fledged U.S. citizens only when their homelands became states.

Despite their quasi-citizenship status, Mexican Americans had the potential to become citizens, a fact that stood in stark contrast to the condition of African Americans and Native Americans, who would not gain this advantage until 1868 and 1887, respectively. By allowing Mexicans to become citizens, the Senate in effect made them white (for legal purposes), since under the provisions of the Naturalization Act of 1790 only whites could become citizens. This was an unstable whiteness, of course, with contingencies, and Mexican Americans would constantly have to fight to secure their rights.

With these changes in place, the Senate ratified the treaty on March 10, 1848, by a vote of 38 to 14 (Document 44). The vote split along sectional, rather than party, lines, thus further foreshadowing the Civil War.

The treaty now had to be approved by the Mexican government. Knowing that the government would not be happy with the Senate's changes, Polk sent two commissioners, Ambrose Sevier and Nathan Clifford, to Mexico. They were to deliver the treaty, explain the alterations, and, most important, accept the treaty's endorsement as soon as it occurred. Sevier and Clifford arrived in Mexico in mid-April, but the Mexican Congress did not begin ratification proceedings until May 3. The Mexican Congress heard from several officials during its ratification debates, including acting president Manuel de la Peña y Peña, who supported ratification (Document 45). Manuel Crescencio Rejón, former minister of the interior and foreign affairs, urged the Mexican Congress to oppose the treaty (Document 46). The treaty faced the greatest opposition from the Chamber of Deputies, which ultimately ratified it by a vote of 51 to 35. Opposition was not as prevalent in the Mexican Senate, which after three days of debate, voted 33 to 4 to ratify. In the end, the Mexican Congress ratified the treaty to ensure that the nation would be free of foreign rule, to prevent further loss of land, and to help the country begin to heal.

Before ratification proceedings began, Mexican foreign relations minister Luis de la Rosa asked the American commissioners to meet with him to clarify the U.S. Senate's intentions in modifying the treaty. From this encounter, the Protocol of Querétaro emerged, which explained the U.S. government's objectives in altering Article IX and striking Article X (Document 47).

In 1853, the Gadsden Purchase secured an additional 29,142,000 acres of Mexican land for the United States. Yet the Gadsden Treaty did not end boundary problems. For the rest of the nineteenth century and into the twentieth, the International Boundary Commission tried to settle disputes between the United States and Mexico over Indian warfare, banditry, smuggling, and invasions by Americans acting on their own without the sanction of the U.S. government.

FOREIGNERS IN THEIR NATIVE LAND

Mexican inhabitants of the ceded territories were now living in the United States and subjected to institutionalized racism. This would further the process of racialization and make Mexican Americans foreigners in their native land. In addition, the United States denied U.S. citizenship to Indians who had been Mexican citizens. Under the 1787 Northwest Ordinance, Indians did not own the land they inhabited, thereby extinguishing their property rights. Given this precedent, at the war's end, the U.S. Congress assumed the authority to validate or invalidate land agreements made by the Mexican government with Indians, including those formerly residing on missions. Mestizos and people of African descent also were affected by racially prejudiced land policies. Each state and territory passed property laws that affected people of color in different ways. This was most evident in how Mexican American property was dealt with in California, New Mexico, and Texas.

California had perhaps the most notorious land legislation. With the discovery of gold there in 1848, the Treaty of Guadalupe Hidalgo's land guarantees were in effect voided. The subsequent gold rush brought thousands of migrants to California. Failing to find precious metals, many encroached on what they perceived to be available land. In truth, it was property granted by the Spanish or Mexican government to Californios. By 1850, California's population had swelled to more than 100,000, with approximately 80,000 Americans, 8,000 Mexicans, 5,000 South Americans, and several thousand newcomers from Europe and Asia. Migrants soon outnumbered the relatively small Californio population of 9,100. The burgeoning American population put California on the fast track to statehood, which it achieved in September 1850.

Despite Articles VIII and IX of the Treaty of Guadalupe Hidalgo, which guaranteed the property and civil rights of Mexicans living in the ceded territory, when American squatters in California demanded that the land be "liberated," the U.S. Congress complied by passing the California Land Act of 1851 (Document 48). This legislation created a three-member board of commissioners to determine the validity of Mexican land grants in California. The commission placed the burden of proof on property owners and mandated that every grantee present evidence confirming his title to the land within two years. Otherwise, the property would pass into the public domain. Underlying these proceedings was a belief that the titles were imperfect and that most of the land grants were in prime spots along the California coast. Eventually, the commission investigated 816 claims and confirmed 604 of them, but the proceedings were a financial burden to titleholders. First, the claimants and their witnesses had to travel to San Francisco, where the commission met (except for a three-month session in Los Angeles in 1852). Second, the claimants had to hire American lawyers to argue their cases before the commission. Lastly, the claimants needed to get copies of the archives concerning their property from the surveyor general's office in San Francisco. These steps often depleted the claimants' funds, and some were forced to mortgage their ranchos to cover the cost of trying to keep their land. These hardships were outlined in a petition sent by fifty-three Californios to the U.S. Senate and House of Representatives in 1859 (Document 49).

Since New Mexico was a territory rather than a state, Congress implemented and oversaw a system of resolving land tenure problems. Compared to California and Texas, New Mexico's population was relatively small. The 1850 U.S. Census reported 67,547 inhabitants in the territory, of which approximately 62,000 were Mexican American, 5,525 were American, and 22 were black. The low number of Americans guaranteed that New Mexico would continue to be a territory rather than becoming a state. (It would gain statehood in 1912.) This, in turn, ensured that the federal government would play a bigger role in property cases there and that Congress, rather than a commission, would confirm titles, making for a longer and more politicized verification process. As opposed to California, where the majority of the claims were confirmed, in New Mexico only 150 of the 1,000 claims filed between 1854 and 1880 were processed.

Because Texas had been a republic before it entered the Union, its way of dealing with land grant confirmation was different from the processes in California and New Mexico. Article 6 of the 1836 Texas Constitution declared that all persons—except Indians and blacks—living in Texas on March 2 of that year (the day that the Texas Declaration of Independence was adopted) could keep the land on which they resided. Those without property would be given some. Two years later, the Texas Congress established the Land Office for the Republic of Texas to investigate Spanish and Mexican land grant claims in areas that were part of the republic at its founding. Since many of the leaders of the republic had been granted land by the Spanish or Mexican government, it was in their interest to secure the titles to their land. To confirm a grant, the claimant had to produce a deed or survey or show that the Mexican government had registered the claim. Once the land office reviewed the claim, the Texas Congress either confirmed or rejected it. When Texas entered the Union, it was able to keep its public land. Thus state laws rather than federal laws proved dominant in settling land disputes.

Not only did many ethnic Mexicans in the ceded territories lose their land, but they also lost their civil rights and were ultimately racialized into an underclass between slaves, free blacks, and whites. Although this phenomenon occurred throughout the Southwest, it was most marked in Texas and California, where more Americans migrated. It is exemplified by the treatment of native San Antonian Juan Seguín, a participant in the Texas War for Independence and eventually the mayor of his hometown. In 1842, when Mexican troops captured San Antonio, the commanding officer invited all Tejanos (ethnic Mexican Texans) to return to Mexico. He also announced publicly that Seguín was still loyal to the old country. That was a lie, but Seguín's enemies used it to question his allegiance to the Lone Star Republic. Although Seguín led troops against the Mexican invaders, public suspicion forced him into hiding. At the same time, volunteers sent by the Republic of Texas to fight the Mexicans occupied the city and harassed Tejano residents by stealing their livestock and corn and in some cases using violence against them. Twenty prominent Tejano families fled their homes. Ultimately, Seguín resigned, left his homeland, and moved to Mexico, the country he had fought against only six years earlier. In his memoirs, Seguín said that he had become "a foreigner in my native land" (Document 50).

Mexican women were discriminated against not just by race but also by gender. Under Mexican law, a woman's property was protected. If she married, any possessions that she held before the marriage were entrusted to her husband to protect and preserve. The same was true of property acquired during the marriage. Once widowed, the woman retained ownership of her dowry and could will it to whomever she chose. After the U.S. takeover, this changed. The American legal system was based on the law of coverture, which dictated that a wife was literally "covered" by her husband, giving him control over her property. He could prevent its sale, lease, or bequest. Under U.S. law, Mexican women became common-law dependents of their husbands, who were deemed the masters of their households. Under Mexican law a husband held his wife's property in trust, and he did not become its owner. He could not sell it or discard it in any way. The U.S. legal system did expand a Mexican woman's ability to escape an unhappy marriage. Previously, a woman's options for charging her spouse with infidelity or other inappropriate behavior in open court were limited. Now she could bring her husband before a tribunal and seek a divorce. Seeking a divorce was risky, however, given that the woman could be deemed dishonorable or, worse, left destitute without any means of support, since her husband could keep her property.

Other forms of discrimination also occurred. In California, following the gold rush, the state legislature passed the Foreign Miners Tax in 1850. This infamous legislation levied a duty on "foreign" prospectors and is a good example of how racism became institutionalized. The law was aimed specifically at Mexican, South American, and Chinese miners, whom American prospectors believed should not be entitled to reaping potential riches in the gold mines. It had the effect of targeting native-born Californians of Mexican descent, in effect rendering them foreigners in their native land. The tax mostly affected northern California, where gold mining was common, but racism was common in southern California, too, as is evident in Francisco Ramírez's editorials for the Los Angeles–based newspaper *El Clamor Público* (Document 51).

While Ramírez made Mexican residents of the Los Angeles area aware of injustices, other Californios used violence to fight inequality. The best examples of this were the exploits of the "social bandits" Joaquín Murrieta and Tiburcio Vásquez. Murrieta and his family arrived in California from Sonora, Mexico, during the gold rush. Once they were there, not only did others take their gold claims, but more tragically, a mob lynched Murrieta's older brother, raped his wife, and left Murrieta for dead. When justice was not forthcoming, he avenged his family by robbing American miners. Between 1851 and 1853, he became so notorious that he was pursued by two separate companies of California rangers. At least forty-one Mexican bandits were thought to be him. Among California's Mexican population, Murrieta emerged as a folk hero who had been driven to a life of crime by social and legal injustice. Eventually, the California legislature hired a former Texas Ranger and his company of twenty men to find Murrieta and kill him. Even after his head was put in a jar and exhibited throughout the state as a deterrent to other potential criminals, many Mexican Americans refused to believe that Murrieta had been executed.

Vásquez waged a similar battle against American migrants. A native of Monterey, Vásquez was the scion of a wealthy family who turned to banditry to resist Americans' displacement of Californios. His career as a bandit began in 1852 when he killed a constable, whom he regarded as a symbol of the new American regime. According to the *Los Angeles Express*, Vásquez wanted to raise $60,000 to, as he allegedly said, "recruit enough arms and men to revolutionize Southern California."[6] Newspapers, most notably the *Los Angeles Star*, followed his exploits (Document 52). For twenty years, Vásquez was in and out of jail. In 1873, he organized a gang that committed crimes throughout the state. A year later, he was captured and charged with murder for a death that had occurred during a robbery. In 1875, he was tried, found guilty, and executed. Because many Mexicans viewed him as a hero, his execution only deepened racial divisions in California.

Mexican Americans also resisted the new regime in peaceful ways. Key among them was actively maintaining their heritage. They celebrated Mexican holidays such as the Sixteenth of September (Mexican Independence Day) and Cinco de Mayo. Commemorating the May 5, 1862, Battle of Puebla, in which a small group of Mexicans fought off an invading French army, Cinco de Mayo held special meaning for Mexicans in the ceded territories, where it was first celebrated in 1863. Although the French occupied Mexico for most of the 1860s, the event symbolized Mexicans' ability to resist an imperialist force. With the recent American takeover of their native lands, Mexican Americans of the Southwest saw parallels between their situation and that of their former compatriots in Puebla.

The celebration of Mexican holidays instilled a pride in Mexican Americans that served as the most important defense against discriminatory practices. This pride led to the development of *mutualistas*, or mutual aid associations. Similar to the mutual assistance and fraternal organizations started by other immigrant groups, *mutualistas* provided ethnic Mexicans[7] with a variety of benefits, including funeral, disability, and other insurance. In so doing, these groups helped bring about a new sense of collective identity. Recognizing that they were not considered full-fledged Americans, many began to see themselves as "Mexicanos" or as members of a larger pan-Hispanic community known as La Raza (the people). These ways of self-identifying have endured to this day. Although there are many differences among Mexican Americans, they still believe that they have much in common with one another. One thing that holds Mexican Americans together is the shared experience of the U.S. war with Mexico, which inspired a legacy of conquest throughout the Southwest that in many ways still treats ethnic Mexicans as foreigners.

MANIFEST DESTINY EXPORTED

Seen through the prism of Indian displacement before and after the U.S. war with Mexico, the conflict emerges as part of a larger U.S. imperial venture in the nineteenth century. It laid the foundation for how the U.S. government would deal with other countries later in the century and into the next. The concept of manifest destiny was a driving force for American expansion abroad in the 1890s, most notably in Hawaii. It not only guaranteed new territory for the United States, but it also ensured commercial markets for American businesses. This was not lost on the *Journal of Commerce and Commercial Bulletin*, which in 1897 reinvigorated the term "manifest destiny" and used it to justify U.S. control of world markets (Document 53). The war also ensured that Mexico would occupy a neocolonial status vis-à-vis the United States. In the twentieth century, the United States invaded Mexico twice[8] and interfered in the affairs of other Latin American countries, including Cuba, Panama, Nicaragua, Guatemala, the Dominican Republic, Chile, and El Salvador, both militarily and economically.

CONCLUSION

The U.S. war with Mexico was a pivotal event in American history that pushed the United States closer to the Civil War by bringing slavery to the political forefront and further dividing the nation along sectional lines, as is evident in the debate over the Wilmot Proviso. As the war progressed, senators and congressmen voted less along partisan lines and more according to pro- or antislavery regional politics. Debates over whether new territories should be free or slave showed how disunified the Union was becoming. In addition, the conflict was a military training ground for men who would become officers in the Civil War, including Robert E. Lee, George McClellan, and Ulysses S. Grant. Equally important, the war lay the foundation for how the United States would wage wars with foreign countries, acquire land, and incorporate new citizens into its fold, while revealing the Republic's deep-seated racial and class dimensions.

Internationally, the war enhanced the strength of the United States on the American continent, creating the basis for its advent as a world power in the next century. It did so at the expense of Mexico, which lost California, with its crucial ports for trade, and Texas, with its vigorous trade, agriculture, and oil-rich land. Perhaps the war's most profound impact was that it created an unequal relationship between the United States and Mexico, which ensured that for 160 years, Mexicans would continuously live on American soil.

NOTES

[1] *New York Herald*, May 21, 1846, 1.

[2] Forced loans were taxes imposed on the richer members of society.

[3] In June 1841, Texas president Mirabal Lamar, without the consent of the republic's congress, initiated the Santa Fe Expedition, an invasion of New Mexico. The expedition was prompted by the president's desire to tap into the trade between Santa Fe and Missouri, which he hoped would not only result in more revenue for the Lone Star Republic, but would give it more leverage within the American continent and allow Texas to fulfill its desire of expansion to the Pacific. However, the New Mexicans, who — contrary to Lamar's belief — did not want to be part of Texas, rebuked, captured, and transported the invaders to Mexico City where they were imprisoned.

[4] A defensive line strategy was the idea of establishing a stationary position that would run along the Rio Grande to the southern border of New Mexico, then west to the head of the Gulf of California, and then turn south to the Pacific Ocean. In this way the United States could terminate fighting, establish the Rio Grande as the border of Texas, and gain a limited amount of territory from Mexico. Calhoun favored this line because it could be easily and inexpensively defended; the area to the north of it was sparsely populated and thus of little value to Mexico, but important to the United States; and finally, it was a way to bring about a permanent and honorable peace.

[5] The Isthmus of Tehauntepec, bordered to the north by the state of Veracruz and to the south by the state of Oaxaca, is the narrowest point in Mexico and the shortest area between the Gulf of Mexico and the Pacific Ocean, and therefore would be beneficial to the U.S. for trade and defense. Another unsuccessful attempt at securing U.S. passage

through the isthmus would occur during the Gadsden Purchase Treaty negotiations in 1853.

[6]Rodolfo Acuña, *Occupied America: A History of Chicanos*, 5th ed. (New York: Longman, 2004), 143.

[7]Ethnic Mexicans denotes Mexican Americans and Mexican immigrants as a whole, and therefore both U.S. citizens and non-U.S. citizens.

[8]In 1914 the United States bombed and invaded Tampico, Veracruz, following a dispute with the government of President Victoriano Huerta. Three years later General John J. Pershing's "punitive expedition" pursued, but never captured, Pancho Villa following his 1916 raid on Columbus, New Mexico.

PART TWO

The Documents

1

JOHN L. O'SULLIVAN

Annexation

July–August 1845

As editor of the New York Morning News *and the* United States Democratic Review, *John L. O'Sullivan first alluded to the notion of manifest
destiny in 1844. It was not until the debate over the annexation of Texas
a year later that he actually coined the phrase and fully articulated it as
a justification for expansionism. The term gained a life of its own when
U.S. representative Robert Winthrop of Massachusetts mocked it in Congress and inadvertently introduced the phrase to a larger audience,
which then used it as a rationale for the war with Mexico.*

It is time now for opposition to the Annexation of Texas to cease, all
further agitation of the waters of bitterness and strife, at least in con-
nexion with this question,—even though it may perhaps be required
of us as a necessary condition of the freedom of our institutions, that

---

From John L. O'Sullivan, "Annexation," *United States Democratic Review*, July–August
1845, 5.

we must live on for ever in a state of unpausing struggle and excitement upon some subject of party division or other. But, in regard to Texas, enough has now been given to Party. It is time for the common duty of Patriotism to the Country to succeed;—or if this claim will not be recognized, it is at least time for common sense to acquiesce with decent grace in the inevitable and the irrevocable.

Texas is now ours. Already, before these words are written, her Convention has undoubtedly ratified the acceptance, by her Congress, of our proffered invitation into the Union; and made the requisite changes in her already republican form of constitution to adopt it to its future federal relations. Her star and her stripe may already be said to have taken their place in the glorious blazon[1] of our common nationality; and the sweep of our eagle's wing already includes within its circuit the wide extent of her fair and fertile land. She is no longer to us a mere geographical space—a certain combination of coast, plain, mountain, valley, forest and stream. She is no longer to us a mere country on the map. She comes within the dear and sacred designation of Our Country; no longer a "*pays*," she is a part of "*la patrie*;" and that which is at once a sentiment and a virtue, Patriotism, already begins to thrill for her too within the national heart. It is time then that all should cease to treat her as alien, and even adverse—cease to denounce and vilify all and everything connected with her accession—cease to thwart and oppose the remaining steps for its consummation; or where such efforts are felt to be unavailing, at least to embitter the hour of reception by all the most ungracious frowns of aversion and words of unwelcome. There has been enough of all this. It has had its fitting day during the period when, in common with every other possible question of practical policy that can arise, it unfortunately became one of the leading topics of party division, of presidential electioneering. But that period has passed, and with it let its prejudices and its passions, its discords and its denunciations, pass away too. The next session of Congress will see the representatives of the new young State in their places in both our halls of national legislation, side by side with those of the old Thirteen. Let their reception into "the family" be frank, kindly, and cheerful, as befits such an occasion, as comports not less with our own self-respect than patriotic duty towards them. Ill betide those foul birds that delight to [de]file their own nest, and disgust the ear with perpetual discord of ill-omened croak.

---

[1]*blazon*: A coat of arms or flag.

Why, were other reasoning wanting, in favor of now elevating this question of the reception of Texas into the Union, out of the lower region of our past party dissensions, up to its proper level of a high and broad nationality, it surely is to be found, found abundantly, in the manner in which other nations have undertaken to intrude themselves into it, between us and the proper parties to the case, in a spirit of hostile interference against us, for the avowed object of thwarting our policy and hampering our power, limiting our greatness and checking the fulfilment of our manifest destiny to overspread the continent allotted by Providence for the free development of our yearly multiplying millions.

2

U.S. CONGRESS

Naturalization Act

March 26, 1790

Enacted by the First Congress, this act established the guidelines for aliens seeking to become naturalized citizens of the United States. It made whiteness mandatory for full American citizenship and set a precedent for incorporating foreigners into the American Republic.

SECTION 1. *Be it enacted by the Senate and House of Representatives of the United States of America in Congress assembled,* That any alien, being a free white person, who shall have resided within the limits and under the jurisdiction of the United States for the term of two years, may be admitted to become a citizen thereof, on application to any common law court of record, in any one of the states wherein he shall have resided for the term of one year at least, and making proof to the satisfaction of such court, that he is a person of good character, and taking the oath or affirmation prescribed by law, to support the

From Richard Peters, ed., *Public Statutes at Large of the United States of America* (Boston: Little, Brown, 1853), 1:103–04.

constitution of the United States, which oath or affirmation such court shall administer; and the clerk of such court shall record such application, and the proceedings thereon; and thereupon such person shall be considered as a citizen of the United States. And the children of such persons so naturalized, dwelling within the United States, being under the age of twenty-one years at the time of such naturalization, shall also be considered as citizens of the United States. And the children of citizens of the United States, that may be born beyond sea, or out of the limits of the United States, shall be considered as natural born citizens: *Provided,* That the right of citizenship shall not descend to persons whose fathers have never been resident in the United States: *Provided also,* That no person heretofore proscribed by any state, shall be admitted a citizen as aforesaid, except by an act of the legislature of the state in which such person was proscribed.

3

AGUSTÍN DE ITURBIDE

Plan de Iguala

February 24, 1821

Issued by Agustín de Iturbide in February 1821, the Plan de Iguala presented his multiracial vision for Mexico while still clinging to traditional vestiges of power. Its guarantees ensured that a coalition of forces would support Mexico's independence from Spain. Most important, the plan showed how Mexican leaders imagined the new nation.

ART. 1.   The Mexican nation is independent of the Spanish nation, and of every other, even on its own Continent.
ART. 2.   Its religion shall be the Catholic, which all its inhabitants profess.

From Biblioteca Enciclopédia Popular, *Documentos de la Guerra de Independencia* (Mexico City: Secretaria de Educación Pública, 1945), 69–73.

ART. 3.   They shall be all united, without any distinction between Americans and Europeans.

ART. 4.   The government shall be a constitutional monarchy.

ART. 5.   A junta shall be named, consisting of, individuals who enjoy the highest reputation in the different parties which have shown themselves.

ART. 6.   This junta shall be under the presidency of his Excellency the Count del Venadito, the present Viceroy of Mexico.

ART. 7.   It shall govern in the name of the nation, according to the laws now in force, and its principal business will be to convoke, according to such rules as it shall deem expedient, a congress for the formation of a constitution more suitable to the country.

ART. 8.   His Majesty Ferdinand VII shall be invited to the throne of the empire, and in case of his refusal, the Infantes Don Carlos and Don Francisco de Paula.

ART. 9.   Should his Majesty Ferdinand VII and his august brothers decline the invitation, the nation is at liberty to invite to the imperial throne any member of reigning families whom it may select.

ART. 10.   The formation of the constitution by the congress, and the oath of the emperor to observe it, must precede his entry into the country.

ART. 11.   The distinction of castes is abolished, which was made by the Spanish law, excluding them from the rights of citizenship. All the inhabitants of the country are citizens, and equal, and the door of advancement is open to virtue and merit.

ART. 12.   An army shall be formed for the support of religion, independence, and union, guaranteeing these three principles, and therefore it shall be called the army of the three guarantees.

ART. 13.   It shall solemnly swear to defend the fundamental bases of this plan.

ART. 14.   It shall strictly observe the military ordinances now in force.

. . .

ART. 24.   It being indispensable to the country that this plan should be carried into effect, in as much as the welfare of that country is its object, every individual of the army shall maintain it, to the shedding (if it be necessary) of the last drop of his blood.

Town of Iguala, 24th February, 1821.

4

MEXICAN CONSTITUTIONAL CONGRESS

Mexican Constitution

1824

Written after the dissolution of the Mexican empire and the establishment of the republic, the Mexican Constitution was similar to its U.S. counterpart. However, unlike the U.S. Constitution, it guaranteed rights to Mexico's population as a whole and was ultimately more far-reaching. Like the Plan de Iguala (Document 3), the Mexican Constitution specified who should be included in Mexico's political community.

In the name of GOD, all powerful, author and supreme legislator of society. The general constituent Congress of the Mexican Nation, in the discharge of the duties confided to them by their constituents, in order to establish and fix its political Independence, establish and confirm its Liberty, and promote its prosperity and glory, decree as follows:

Constitution of the United Mexican States

TITLE 1ST. ONLY SECTION.—*Of the Mexican Nation, its Territory and Religion.*
ARTICLE 1.   The Mexican Nation, is forever free and independent of the Spanish government, and every other power.

   2. Its Territory consists of that, which was formerly called the viceroyalty of New-Spain, that styled the captain generalship of Tucaton, that of the commandant generalship formerly called the Internal Provinces of East and West, and that of Lower and Upper Caliafornia [*sic*], with the lands annexed, and adjacent lands in both seas. By a constitutional law, a demarkation of the limits of the Federation will be made as soon as circumstances will permit.

From David B. Edward, *The History of Texas*, Brasada Reprint Series (Austin, Tex.: Pemberton Press, 1967), 322–23.

3. The Religion of the Mexican Nation, is, and will be perpetually, the Roman Catholic Apostolic. The Nation will protect it by wise and just laws, and prohibit the exercise of any other whatever.

TITLE 2D. ONLY SECTION.—*Form of Government of the Nation, of its integral parts and division of Supreme Power.*

4. The Mexican Nation adopts for its Government, the form of Republican representative, popular Federal.

5. The parts of this Federation, are the States and Territories as follows:—The State of the Chiapas, Chiuahua, Coahuila and Texas, Durango, Guanajuato, Mexico, Michoacan, New Leon, Oajaca, Puebla de los Angeles, Quetaro [*sic*], San Luis Potosi, Sinora and Sinaloa, Tobasco, Tumaulipas [*sic*], Vera Cruz, Xalisco, Yucatan Tacatecas [*sic*]; the Territory of Upper Caliafornia, Lower Caliafornia, Colima and Sante Fe of New Mexico—a constitutional law shall fix the character of Tlaxcala.

6. The supreme power of the Federation will be divided for its exercises, in Legislative, Executive, and Judicial.

TITLE 3D. SECTION 1ST.—*Legislative power, of its nature and the mode of exercising it.*

7. The legislative power of the Federation, shall be disposed in a General Congress, this to be divided in two houses, one of Deputies (Representatives) and the other of Senators.

SECTION 2D.—*Of the House of Representatives.*

. . .

19. To be a Representative it is required—First, To be at the time of the election, twenty-five years of age, complete. Second, To have been a resident of the State, from which elected, at least two years, or born in the State, although a resident in another.

20. Those not born in the territory of the Mexican Nation, to be Representatives, must have, besides eight years' residence in it, 8,000 dollars of real estate in any part of the Republic, or an occupation that produces them 1,000 per year.

5

U.S. CONGRESS

Indian Removal Act

May 28, 1830

After bitter debate, Congress passed this act allowing President Andrew Jackson to remove Indian nations from any state or territory in exchange for western land. The act enabled the president to carry out his planned removal of the southeastern tribes to the West and set the precedent for legislation that would eventually remove ethnic Mexicans from their land following the U.S. war with Mexico.

Be it enacted by the Senate and House of Representatives of the United States of America, in Congress assembled, That it shall and may be lawful for the President of the United States to cause so much of any territory belonging to the United States, west of the river Mississippi, not included in any state or organized territory, and to which the Indian title has been extinguished, as he may judge necessary, to be divided into a suitable number of districts, for the reception of such tribes or nations of Indians as may choose to exchange the lands where they now reside, and remove there; and to cause each of said districts to be so described by natural or artificial marks, as to be easily distinguished from every other.

SEC. 2. *And be it further enacted,* That it shall and may be lawful for the President to exchange any or all of such districts, so to be laid off and described, with any tribe or nation of Indians now residing within the limits of any of the states or territories, and with which the United States have existing treaties, for the whole or any part or portion of the territory claimed and occupied by such tribe or nation, within the bounds of any one or more of the states or territories, where the land claimed and occupied by the Indians, is owned by the United States, or the United States are bound to the state within which it lies to extinguish the Indian claim thereto.

From Richard Peters, ed., *Public Statutes at Large of the United States of America* (Boston: Charles C. Little and James Brown, 1846), 4:411–12.

SEC. 3. *And be it further enacted*, That in the making of any such exchange or exchanges, it shall and may be lawful for the President solemnly to assure the tribe or nation with which the exchange is made, that the United States will forever secure and guaranty to them, and their heirs or successors, the country so exchanged with them; and if they prefer it, that the United States will cause a patent or grant to be made and executed to them for the same: *Provided always*, That such lands shall revert to the United States, if the Indians become extinct, or abandon the same.

SEC. 4. *And be it further enacted*, That if, upon any of the lands now occupied by the Indians, and to be exchanged for, there should be such improvements as add value to the land claimed by any individual or individuals of such tribes or nations, it shall and may be lawful for the President to cause such value to be ascertained by appraisement or otherwise, and to cause such ascertained value to be paid to the person or persons rightfully claiming such improvements. And upon the payment of such valuation, the improvements so valued and paid for, shall pass to the United States, and possession shall not afterwards be permitted to any of the same tribe.

SEC. 5. *And be it further enacted*, That upon the making of any such exchange as is contemplated by this act, it shall and may be lawful for the President to cause such aid and assistance to be furnished to the emigrants as may be necessary and proper to enable them to remove to, and settle in, the country for which they may have exchanged; and also, to give them such aid and assistance as may be necessary for their support and subsistence for the first year after their removal.

SEC. 6. *And be it further enacted*, That it shall and may be lawful for the President to cause such tribe or nation to be protected, at their new residence, against all interruption or disturbance from any other tribe or nation of Indians, or from any other person or persons whatever.

SEC. 7. *And be it further enacted*, That it shall and may be lawful for the President to have the same superintendence and care over any tribe or nation in the country to which they may remove, as contemplated by this act, that he is now authorized to have over them at their present places of residence: *Provided*, That nothing in this act contained shall be construed as authorizing or directing the violation of any existing treaty between the United States and any of the Indian tribes.

SEC. 8. *And be it further enacted*, That for the purpose of giving effect to the provisions of this act, the sum of five hundred thousand dollars is hereby appropriated, to be paid out of any money in the treasury, not otherwise appropriated.

6

UNITED STATES AND KINGDOM OF SPAIN

Treaty of San Lorenzo

October 27, 1795

This accord not only established U.S. diplomatic relations with the Spanish kingdom but also set the boundaries between the two countries' territories. It would be the first of many agreements aimed at securing the United States' southern border. In the context of the U.S. war with Mexico, the Treaty of San Lorenzo demonstrates the American government's long-standing preoccupation with demarcating its southern border.

His Catholic Majesty and the United States of America desiring to consolidate on a permanent basis the Friendship and good correspondence which happily prevails between the two Parties, have determined to establish by a convention several points, the settlement whereof will be productive of general advantage and reciprocal utility to both Nations. . . .

Art. I.   There shall be a firm and inviolable Peace and sincere Friendship between His Catholic Majesty his successors and subjects, and the United [States] and their Citizens without exception of persons or places.

Art. II.   To prevent all disputes on the subject of the boundaries which separate the territories of the two High contracting Parties, it is hereby declared and agreed as follows: to wit: The Southern boundary of the United States which divides their territory from the Spanish Colonies of East and West Florida, shall be designated by a line beginning on the River Mississipi at the Northermost part of the thirty-first degree of latitude North of the Equator, which from thence shall be drawn due East to the middle of the River Apalachicola or Catabouche, thence along the middle thereof to its junction with the Flint, thence straight to the head of St. Mary's River, and thence down the middle there of to the Atlantic [Ocean]. And it is agreed that if there

From David Hunter Miller, ed., *Treaties and Other International Acts of the United States of America* (Washington, D.C.: Government Printing Office, 1937), 2:318–23.

should be any troops, Garrisons or settlements of either Party in the territory of the other according to the above mentioned boundaries, they shall be withdrawn from the said territory within the term of six months after the ratification of this treaty or sooner if it be possible and that they shall be permitted to take with them all the goods and effects which they possess.

. . .

ART. IV.   It is likewise agreed that the Western boundary of the United States which separates them from the Spanish Colony of [Louisiana], is in the middle of the channel or bed of the River Mississip[p]i from the Northern boundary of the said States to the completion of the thirty-first degree of latitude North of the Equator; and his Catholic Majesty has likewise agreed that the navigation of the said River in its whole breadth from its source to the [Ocean] shall be free only to his Subjects, and the Citizens of the United States, unless he should extend this privilege to the Subjects of other Powers by special convention.

7

UNITED STATES AND FRANCE

Louisiana Purchase Treaty

April 30, 1803

With this accord, the United States bought Louisiana from France and in so doing incorporated French citizens living there into the American Republic. The treaty set a precedent for the manner in which citizens of another country would be integrated into the United States. It would eventually become the basis for Article IX of the Treaty of Guadalupe Hidalgo.

From David Hunter Miller, ed., *Treaties and Other International Acts of the United States of America* (Washington, D.C.: Government Printing Office, 1937), 2:498–501.

Treaty between the United States of America and the French Republic

ARTICLE I. Whereas by the Article the third of the Treaty concluded at St. Idelfonso the . . . 1st October 1800 between the First Consul of the French Republic and his Catholic Majesty it was agreed as follows.

"His Catholic Majesty promises and engages on his part to cede to the French Republic six months after the full and entire execution of the conditions and Stipulations herein relative to his Royal Highness the Duke of Parma, the Colony or Province of Louisiana with the Same extent that it now has in the hands of Spain, & that it had when France possessed it; and Such as it Should be after the Treaties subsequ[e]ntly entered into between Spain and other States."

And whereas in pursuance of the Treaty and particularly of the third article the French Republic has an incontestible title to the domain and to the possession of the said Territory—The First Consul of the French Republic desiring to give to the United States a strong proof of his friendship doth hereby cede to the said United States in the name of the French Republic for ever and in full Sovereignty the said territory with all its rights and appurtenances as full and in the Same manner as they have been acquired by the French Republic in virtue of the above mentioned Treaty concluded with his Catholic Majesty.

ART. II. In the cession made by the preceding article are included the adjacent Islands belonging to Louisiana all public lots and Squares, vacant lands and all public buildings, fortifications, barracks and other edifices which are not private property.—The Archives, papers & documents relative to the domain and Sovereignty of Louisiana and its dependances will be left in the possession of the Commissaries of the United States, and copies will be afterwards given in due form to the Magistrates and Municipal officers of Such of the said papers and documents as may be necessary to them.

ART. III. The inhabitants of the ceded territory shall be incorporated in the Union of the United States and admitted as soon as possible according to the principles of the federal Constitution to the enjoyment of all the rights, advantages and immunities of citizens of the United States, and in the mean time they shall be maintained and protected in the free enjoyment of their liberty, property and the Religion which they profess.

8

MEXICAN GOVERNMENT

National Colonization Law

August 18, 1824

Predating the Mexican Constitution by two months, the colonization law offered foreigners the opportunity to immigrate to Mexico. Though extending to the entire nation, the act was aimed at populating Mexico's northern provinces both as a defensive strategy and a nation-building vehicle. Note the lax stipulations for colonization.

The Supreme Executive Power, provisionally appointed by the General Sovereign Constituent Congress—To all who shall see and understand these presents: know ye—that the said Congress, has decreed as follows:

ART. 1.   The Mexican nation offers to foreigners, who come to establish themselves within its territory, security for their persons and property, provided, they subject themselves to the laws of the country.

ART. 2.   This law comprehends those lands of the nation, not the property of individuals, corporations, or towns, which can be colonized.

ART. 3.   For this purpose the Legislature of the States, will, as soon as possible, form colonization laws, or regulations for their respective states, conforming themselves in all things, to the constitutional act, general constitution, and the regulations established in this law.

ART. 4.   There cannot be colonized any lands, comprehended within twenty leagues of the limits of any foreign nation, nor within ten leagues of the coasts, without the previous approbation of the general supreme executive power.

ART. 5.   If for the defence and security of the nation, the federal government should deem it necessary to use any portion of these lands, for the construction of warehouses, arsenals, or other public edifices,

From Ernest Wallace and David M. Vignesis, eds., *Documents of the Republic of Texas* (Austin, Tex.: State House Press, 1963), 48.

they can do so, with the approbation of the general congress, or in its recess, of the council of government.

ART. 6.   Until after four years from the publication of this law, there shall not be imposed any tax whatever, on the entrance of foreigners, who come to establish themselves for the first time, in the nation.

ART. 7.   Until after the year 1840, the general congress shall not prohibit the entrance of any foreigner, as a colonist, unless imperious circumstances should require it, with respect to the individuals of a particular nation.

ART. 8.   The government, without prejudicing the objects of this law, shall take such precautionary measures as it may deem expedient, for the security of the confederation, as respects the foreigners who come to colonize.

ART. 9.   A preference shall be given in the distribution of lands, to Mexican citizens, and no other distinction shall be made in regard to them except that which is founded on individual merit, or services rendered the country, or under equal circumstances, a residence in the place where the lands to be distributed are situated.

ART. 10.   The military who in virtue of the offer made on the 27th March, 1821, have a right to lands, shall be attended to by the states, in conformity with the diplomas which are issued to that effect, by the supreme executive power.

ART. 11.   If in virtue of the decree alluded to, in the last article, and taking into view the probabilities of life, the supreme executive power should deem it expedient to alienate any portion of land in favor of any officer, whether civil or military of the federation, it can do so from the vacant lands of the territories.

ART. 12.   It shall not be permitted to unite in the same hands with the right of property, more than one league square of land, suitable for irrigation, four square leagues in superficie,[1] of arable land without the facilities of irrigation, and six square leagues in superficie of grazing land.

ART. 13.   The new colonists shall not transfer their property in mortmain (*manus muertos*).[2]

ART. 14.   This law guarantees the contracts which the empresarios[3]

---

[1] *superficie*: The extent or size of a flat surface.
[2] *mortmain* (manus muertos): The possession of real property in perpetuity by a corporate body.
[3] *empresario*: A land agent or land contractor.

make with the families which they bring at their own expense, provided they are not contrary to the laws.

ART. 15.   No person who by virtue of this law, acquires a title to lands, shall hold them if he is domiciliated[4] out of the limits of the republic.

ART. 16.   The government in conformity with the provisions established in this law, will proceed to colonize the territories of the republic.

[4]*domiciliated*: Living or establishing a residency.

9

LEGISLATURE OF COAHUILA-TEXAS

Coahuila-Texas State Colonization Law
March 24, 1825

Designed to augment the National Colonization Law and specifically regulate immigration into Coahuila-Texas, this legislation refined the stipulations of the national law by offering further incentives for settlement in the northern state. Notice the law's stringent guidelines and consider how Coahuila-Texas would enforce them.

The Governor provisionally appointed by the Sovereign Congress of this state—to all who shall see these presents; know,—that the said congress, have decreed as follows:—

DECREE NO. 16.   The constituent congress of the free, independent and sovereign State of Coahuila and Texas, desiring by every possible means, to augment the population of its territory; promote the cultivation of its fertile lands; the raising and multiplication of stock, and the progress of the arts, and commerce; and being governed by the constitutional act, the federal constitution, and the basis established by the national decree of the general congress, No. 72, have thought proper to decree the following LAW OF COLONIZATION:

From Ernest Wallace and David M. Vignesis, eds., *Documents of the Republic of Texas* (Austin, Tex.: State House Press, 1963), 48.

ART. 1. All foreigners, who in virtue of the general laws of the 18th. August, 1824, which guarantees the security of their persons and property, in the territory of the Mexican nation, wish to remove to any of the settlements of the state of Coahuila and Texas, are at liberty to do so; and the said state invites and calls them.

ART. 2. Those who do so instead of being incommoded,[1] shall be admitted by the local authorities of said settlements, who shall freely permit them to pursue any branch of industry, that they may think proper, provided they respect the general laws of the nation, and those of the state.

. . .

ART. 5. Foreigners of any nation, or a native of any of the Mexican states, can project the formation of new towns on any lands entirely vacant, or even on those of an individual, in the case mentioned in the 35th article; but the new settlers who present themselves for admission, must prove their [C]hristianity, morality, and good habits, by a certificate from the authorities where they formerly resided. . . .

ART. 7. The government shall take care, that within the twenty leagues bordering on the limits of the United States of the North, and ten leagues in a straight line from the coast of the Gul[f] of Mexico, within the limits of this state, there shall be no other settlements, except such as merit the approbation of the supreme government of the Union, for which object, all petitions on the subject, whether made by Mexicans or foreigners, shall be passed to the superior government, accompanied by a corresponding report.

. . .

ART. 19. The Indians of all nations, bordering on the state, as well as wandering tribes that may be within its limits, . . . after having first declared themselves in favor of our religion and institutions wish to establish themselves in any settlements that are forming, they shall be admitted, and the same quantity of land given them, as to the settlers, spoken of in the 14th. and 15th. articles, always preferring native Indians to strangers.

. . .

---

[1]*incommoded*: Inconvenienced, disturbed.

ART. 22. The new settlers as an acknowledgment, shall pay to the state, for each sitio[2] of pasture land, thirty dollars; two dollars and a half, for each [area] without the facility of irrigation, and three dollars and a half, for each one that can be irrigated, and so on proportionally according to the quantity and quality of the land distributed; but the said payments need not be made, until six years after the settlement, and by thirds; the first within four years, the second within five years, and the last within six years, under the penalty of losing the land, for a failure, in any of said payments. . . .

. . .

ART. 24. The government will sell to Mexicans, and to them only, such lands as they may wish to purchase, taking care that there shall not be accumulated in the same hands more than eleven sitios; and under the condition, that the purchaser must cultivate what he acquires by this title within six years from its acquisition, under the penalty of losing them; the price of each sitio, subject to the foregoing condition, shall be one hundred dollars, if it be pasture land; one hundred and fifty dollars, if it be farming land without the facility of irrigation; and two hundred dollars if it can be irrigated.

ART. 25. Until six years after the publication of this law, the legislature of this state, cannot alter it as regards the acknowledgment, and price to be paid for land, or as regards the quantity and quality, to be distributed to the new settlers, or sold to Mexicans.

ART. 26. The new settlers, who within six years from the date of the possession, have not cultivated or occupied the lands granted them, according to its quality, shall be considered to have renounced them, and the respective political authority, shall immediately proceed to take possession of them, and recall the titles.

. . .

ART. 31. Foreigners who in conformity with this law, have obtained land, and established themselves in any new settlement, shall be considered from that moment, naturalized in the country; and by marrying a Mexican, they acquire a particular merit to obtain letters of citizenship of the state, subject however to the provisions which may be made relative to both particulars, in the constitution of the state.

ART. 32. During the first ten years, counting from the day on which

[2]*sitio*: Place or area.

the new settlements may have been established, they shall be free from all contributions, of whatever denomination, with the exception of those which, in case of invasion by any enemy, or to prevent it, are generally imposed, and all the produce of agriculture or industry of the new settlers, shall be free from excise duty *Alcabala*,[3] or other duties, throughout every part of the state, with the exception of the duties referred to in the next article; after the termination of that time, the new settlements shall be on the same footing as to taxes, with the old ones, and the colonists shall also in this particular, be on the same footing with the other inhabitants of the state.

ART. 33.   From the day of their settlement, the new colonists shall be at liberty to follow any branch of industry, and can also work mines of every description, communicating with the supreme government of the confederation, relative to the general revenue appertaining to it, and subjecting themselves in all other particulars, to the ordinances or taxes, established or which may be established on this branch.

. . .

ART. 42.   Foreigners are eligible, subject to the provisions which the constitution of the state may prescribe, to elect the members of their municipal authorities, and to be elected to the same.

[3] *Alcabala*: Ten percent sales tax (traditionally levied in Castile, Spain).

10

MANUEL MIER Y TERÁN

Letter to War Department
November 29, 1829

Sent to Texas in 1828 to survey the state of affairs there, General Manuel Mier y Terán addressed this personal letter detailing the social conditions in Mexico's northern province to the Mexican minister of war. His suggestions influenced the Mexican government to limit American

From Ohland Morton, *Terán and Texas: A Chapter in Texas-Mexican Relations* (Austin: Texas State Historical Association, 1948), 99–101.

*immigration to Texas in April 1830 and caused tensions that would lead
to the establishment of the Lone Star Republic. Note the letter's tone and
the way Texans are described.*

In reply to the supreme order of October 28, which you sent me relative to an expedition to be made into Texas, I have the honor to inform your Excellency that this is a matter of serious importance, interest, and at present, the most costly to the Mexican federation, and for that reason demands from me a manifestation to the Supreme Government which I ask your Excellency to consider very carefully that it may contribute to the national prosperity, to the conservation of national territory, to the lustre of the President and to the individual honor of his ministers.

The department of Texas is contiguous to the most avid nation in the world. The North Americans have conquered whatever territory adjoins them. In less than half a century, they have become masters of extensive colonies which formerly belonged to Spain and France, and of even more spacious territories from which have disappeared the former owners, the Indian tribes. There is no Power like that to the north, which by silent means, has made conquests of momentous importance. Such dexterity, such constancy in their designs, such uniformity of means of execution which always are completely successful, arouses admiration. Instead of armies, battles, or invasions, which make a great noise and for the most part are unsuccessful, these men lay hands on means, which, if considered one by one, would be rejected as slow, ineffective, and at times palpably absurd. They begin by assuming rights, as in Texas, which it is impossible to sustain in a serious discussion, making ridiculous pretensions based on historical incidents which no one admits—such as the voyage of La Salle, which was an absurd fiasco, but serves as a basis for their claim to Texas. Such extravagant claims as these are now being presented for the first time to the public by dissembling writers; the efforts that others make to submit proofs and reasons are by these men employed in reiterations and in enlarging upon matters of administration in order to attract the attention of their fellow-countrymen, not to the justice of the claim, but to the profit to be gained from admitting it. At this stage it is alleged that there is a national demand for the step which the government meditates. In the meantime, the territory against which these machinations are directed, and which has usually remained unsettled, begins to be visited by adventurers and *empresarios*, some of these take up their residence in the country, pretending that their location has no bearing upon the question of their government's claim or the boundary disputes; shortly, some of these forerunners develop an interest which complicates the political administration of the coveted territory; complaints, even threats, begin to be heard, working on the loyalty of the legitimate settlers, discrediting the efficiency of the existing authority and administration; and the matter having arrived at this stage—which is precisely that of Texas at this moment—diplomatic maneuvers begin: They incite uprisings in the territory in question and usually manifest a deep concern for the rights of the inhabitants. There follows a matter of notes in which are found equitable and moderate phrases, until with the aid of other incidents, which are never lacking in the course of diplomatic relations, comes finally the desired conclusion of a transaction as onerous for one side as advantageous for the other. They used such a method to dispossess the Powers of Europe of vast territories, which under the name of colonies, they once possessed in America, but which were of secondary interest. The question with respect to Mexico is quite different. It is a matter of attacking primary interests intimately tied up with the political existence of our country. Mexico, imitating the conduct of France and Spain, might alienate or cede unproductive lands in Africa or Asia. But, how can it be expected to cut itself off from its own soil, give up to a rival Power territory advantageously placed in the extremity of its states, which joins some of them and serves as a buffer to all? How can it be expected to alienate two hundred and fifty leagues of coast, leaving on them vast resources for the construction of boats, the shortest channels for commerce and navigation, the most fertile lands, and the most copious elements for providing means of attack and defense? If Mexico should consent to this base act, it would degenerate from the most elevated class of the American Powers to that of a contemptible mediocrity, reduced to the necessity of buying a precarious existence at the cost of many humiliations. In the act of ceding Texas it would have to renounce all pretensions of having its own industries with which to maintain and enrich its eight million inhabitants, who within a few years could not avoid seeing the bread and sugar, and even the maize and beans consumed in the federal district, furnished by the foreign harvest of Texas. The sale of this department would reduce the territorial property, it would reduce the value of land in all the rest of Mexico by one-half of that which it now has. These assertions, which carry their own evidence, should be manifest to such an extent, as space will not permit my enlarging upon them, that they will establish a conviction in every

Mexican heart that he who consents to and does not oppose the loss of Texas is an execrable traitor who ought to be punished with every kind of death.

Coming now to the measures which your Excellency ordered for the security of Texas, I have the honor to inform your Excellency that I do not have at my disposal a suitable corps for an immediate expedition. . . .

If war should break out, it would be expedient to suppress it in a single campaign—a less expensive method than to be always on the defensive. But even this would be useless until a colony of one thousand native Mexican families is planted there, an economical measure when it is remembered that the funds spent once in establishing a colony would be spent many times in maintaining garrisons.

11

BENJAMIN LUNDY

Conditions for African Americans in Mexican Texas

1833

A noted Philadelphia abolitionist and mentor to fellow antislavery activist William Lloyd Garrison, Lundy traveled through Mexican Texas to investigate the feasibility of establishing a colony of free African Americans in the state. Eventually, the governor of Coahuila-Texas granted him land along the Nueces–Rio Grande strip, but his efforts were rendered obsolete once Texas gained its independence. Note Lundy's discussion about the African American man he met on his travels.

The town of Bexar contains about two thousand inhabitants. Many of the buildings are of stone, and very lofty, with flat roofs. The larger portion however, are mere huts, constructed principally of poles, with one end set in the ground, in the form of picket-fence. These huts are

From Thomas Earle, ed., *Life, Travels and Opinions of Benjamin Lundy* (New York: Arno Press, 1969), 48–49.

thatched with a kind of coarse grass, and are entirely destitute of floors. . . . I rose early and walked about the town. Many of the people were stirring by daylight, while others were lying on their pallets in front of their houses, it being customary with numbers of the labouring class to sleep in the open air. I called again upon Padilla[1] and showed him my credentials, with which he was quite pleased. He accompanied me on a visit to the authorities of the place. We went first to the political chief, and showed him my passport. He is rather a pleasant man, and speaks pretty good English. We next visited the Alcalde,[2] who took a copy of the passport.—Then I spent the rest of the day in looking about town. There lives here, in Bexar, a free black man, who speaks English. He came as a slave, first from North Carolina to Georgia, and then from Georgia to Nacogdoches, in Texas. There his master died, and the heirs sold him to another person. This new master, being apprehended for debt, offered the slave his freedom if he would take him out of prison. The slave complied, but the master dying soon after, an attempt was made by his heirs to re-enslave the man, which however proved unsuccessful. He now works as a blacksmith in this place. I have been to converse with him, he having seen me at Nacogdoches last summer, and knowing me again when he met me here. He is highly pleased with my plans. Though he is jet-black, he says the Mexicans pay him the same respect as to other laboring people, there being no difference made here on account of colour. Padilla says it is the policy of the Mexican Government to unite all colours and treat all with respect. The Mexicans, in this region, make as good an appearance as any people; but there are very few among them that we should call white. The inhabitants of Bexar appear far better in general than those of Brazoria, San Felipe or Gonzales. They have graceful manners and honest countenances, and exhibit tokens of wealth and independence. Both men and women are fine looking people;—less vivacious than the [Haitians], but more mild and easy in their manners.

---

[1] Juan Antonio Padilla, former secretary of state of Coahuila, Texas.
[2] *Alcalde*: The chief administrator of a town.

12

TEXAN CONSULTATION OF REPRESENTATIVES

Texas Declaration of Independence
March 2, 1836

---

*Issued on March 2, 1836, at Washington-on-the-Brazos by the Texan
Consultation of Representatives, the Texas Declaration of Independence
outlined the grievances leading to the establishment of the Lone Star
Republic.*

The Unanimous
Declaration of Independence
made by the
Delegates of the People of Texas
in
General Convention at the town of Washington
On the 2nd day of March 1836.

When a government has ceased to protect the lives, liberty and property of the people, from whom its legitimate powers are derived, and
for the advancement of whose happiness it was instituted; and so far
from being a guarantee for their inestimable and inalienable rights,
becomes an instrument in the hands of evil rulers for their oppression. . . .

. . . In such a crisis, the first law of nature, the right of self-preservation, the inherent and inalienable right of the people to appeal to first
principles, and take their political affairs into their own hands in
extreme cases, enjoins it as a right towards themselves, and a sacred
obligation to their posterity, to abolish such government, and create
another in its stead, calculated to rescue them from impending dangers, and to secure their welfare and happiness.

Nations, as well as individuals, are amenable for their acts to the
public opinion of mankind. A statement of a part of our grievances is

---

From John Jenkins, ed., *The Papers of the Texas Revolution, 1835–1836* (Austin, Tex.:
Presidial Press, 1973), 4:493–96.

therefore submitted to an impartial world, in justification of the haz-
ardous but unavoidable step now taken, of severing our political
connection with the Mexican people, and assuming an independent
attitude among the nations of the earth.

The Mexican government, by its colonization laws, invited and
induced the Anglo American population of Texas to colonize its wilder-
ness under the pledged faith of a written constitution, that they should
continue to enjoy that constitutional liberty and republican government to which they had been habituated in the land of their birth, the
United States of America.

In this expectation they have been cruelly disappointed, inasmuch
as the Mexican nation has acquiesced to the late changes made in the
government by General Antonio Lopez de Santa Anna, who, having
overturned the constitution of his country, now offers, as the cruel
alternative, either to abandon our homes, acquired by so many privations, or submit to the most intolerable of all tyranny, the combined
despotism of the sword and the priesthood.

It hath sacrificed our welfare to the state of Coahuila, by which our
interests have been continually depressed through a jealous and partial course of legislation, carried on at a far distant seat of government,
by a hostile majority, in an unknown tongue, and this too, notwithstanding we have petitioned in the humblest terms for the establishment of a separate state government, and have, in accordance with the
provisions of the national constitution, presented to the general congress a republican constitution, which was, without a just cause, con-
temptuously rejected.

It incarcerated in a dungeon, for a long time, one of our citizens, for
no other cause but a zealous endeavour to procure the acceptance of
our constitution, and the establishment of a state government.

It has failed and refused to secure, on a firm basis, the right of trial
by jury, that palladium[1] of civil liberty, and only safe guarantee for the
life, liberty, and property of the citizen. . . .

It denies us the right of worshipping the Almighty according to the
dictates of our own conscience, by the support of a national religion,
calculated to promote the temporal interest of its human functionaries,
rather than the glory of the true and living God.

It has demanded us to deliver up our arms, which are essential to
our defence — the rightful property of freemen — and formidable only
to tyrannical governments.

---

[1]*palladium*: A safeguard viewed as a guarantee of the integrity of social institutions.

MESSAGE TO THE INHABITANTS OF TEXAS

It has invaded our country both by sea and by land, with the intent to lay waste our territory, and drive us from our homes; and has now a large mercenary army advancing, to carry on against us a war of extermination. . . .

The necessity of self-preservation, therefore, now decrees our eternal political separation.

We, therefore, the delegates, with plenary powers, of the people of Texas, in solemn convention assembled, appealing to a candid world for the necessities of our condition, do hereby resolve and declare, that our political connection with the Mexican nation has forever ended, and that the people of Texas do now constitute a free, sovereign, and independent republic, and are fully invested with all the rights and attributes which properly belong to independent nations; and, conscious of the rectitude of our intentions, we fearlessly and confidently commit the issue to the supreme Arbiter of the destinies of nations.

13

ANTONIO LÓPEZ DE SANTA ANNA

Message to the Inhabitants of Texas
March 7, 1836

Issued after Santa Anna entered Texas, this pronouncement presented his estimation of the situation in Texas. The decree's main purpose was to inspire Texas's Mexican inhabitants to unite against the independence struggle.

THE GENERAL-IN-CHIEF OF THE ARMY OF OPERATIONS OF THE MEXICAN REPUBLIC, TO THE INHABITANTS OF TEXAS:
Citizens! The causes which have conducted to this frontier a part of the Mexican army are not unknown to you: a parcel of aud[a]cious

From John Jenkins, ed., *The Papers of the Texas Revolution, 1835–1836* (Austin, Tex.: Presidial Press, 1973), 4:20–21.

adventurers, maliciously protected by some inhabitants of a neighboring republic, dared to invade our territory, with an intention of dividing amongst themselves the fertile lands that are contained in the spacious department of Texas; and even had the boldness to entertain the idea of reaching the capital of the Republic. It became necessary to check and chastise such enormous daring; and in consequence, some exemplary punishments have already taken place in Saint Patrick, Lipantitlan and this city. I am pained to find amongst those adventurers the names of some colonists, to whom had been granted repeated benefits, and who had no just motive of complaint against the government of their adopted country.—These ungrateful men must also necessarily suffer the just punishment that the laws and the public vengeance demand. But if we are found to punish the criminal, we are not the less compelled to protect the innocent. It is thus that the inhabitants of this country, let their origin be whatever it may, who should not appear to have been implicated in such iniquitous rebellion, shall be respected in their persons and property, provided they come forward and report themselves to the commander of the troops within eight days after they should have arrived in their respective settlements, in order to justify their conduct and to receive a document guaranteeing to them the right of enjoying that which lawfully belongs to them.

Bexarians! Return to your homes and dedicate yourselves to your domestic duties. Your city and the fortress of the Alamo are already in possession of the Mexican army, composed of you[r] own fellow citizens; and rest assured that no mass of foreigners will ever interrupt your repose, and much less, attack your lives and plunder your property. The supreme government has taken you under its protection, and will seek for your good.

Inhabitants of Texas! I have related to you the orders that the army of operations I have the honor to command comes to execute; and therefore the good will have nothing to fear. Fulfill always your duties as Mexican citizens, and you may expect the protection and benefit of the laws; and rest assured that you will never have reason to report yourselves of having observed such conduct, for I pledge you in the name of the supreme authorities of the nation, and as your fellow citizen and friend, that what has been promised you will be faithfully performed.

Antonio López de Santa Anna.

14

EULALIA YORBA

Another Story of the Alamo: The Battle Described by an Alleged Eyewitness

April 1896

Thirty-four years old at the time of the battle, Eulalia Yorba relayed her recollections about the event and its aftermath to the San Antonio Express *in 1896.*

Along about nine o'clock, I should judge, the shooting and swearing and yelling had ceased, but the air was thick and heavy with blue powder smoke. A Mexican colonel came running to the priest's residence and asked that we go down to the Alamo to do what we could for the dying men.

Such a dreadful sight. The roadway was thronged with Mexican soldiers with smoke and dirt begrimed faces, haggard eyes and wild, insane expression. There were twelve or fifteen bodies of Mexicans lying dead and bleeding here and there and others were being carried to an adobe house across the way. The stones in the church wall were spotted with blood, the doors were splintered and battered in. Pools of thick blood were so frequent on the sun-baked earth about the stone building that we had to be careful to avoid stepping in them. There was a din of excited voices along the street and the officers were marshaling their men for moving to camp.

But no one could even tell you the horror of the scene that met our gaze when we were led by the sympathetic little colonel into the old Alamo to bandage up the wounds of several young men there. I used to try when I was younger to describe that awful sight, but I never could find sufficient language. There were only a few Mexicans in there when we came and they were all officers who had ordered the common soldiers away from the scene of death and—yes—slaughter,

San Antonio Express, April 12, 1896. Reprinted from Timothy M. Matovina, ed., *The Alamo Remembered: Tejano Accounts and Perspectives* (Austin: University of Texas Press, 1995), 56–57.

for that was what it was. The floor was literally crimson with blood. The woodwork all about us was riddled and splintered by lead balls and what was left of the old altar at the rear of the church was cut and slashed by cannon ball[s] and bullets. The air was dark with powder smoke and was hot and heavy. The odor was oppressive and sickening and the simply horrible scene [un]nerved us as nothing else could.

The dead Texans lay singly and in heaps of three or four, or in irregular rows here and there all about the floor of the Alamo, just as they had fallen when a ball reached a vital part or they had dropped to their death from loss of blood. Of course we went to work as soon as we got to the mission at helping the bleeding and moaning men, who had only a few hours at most more of life; but the few minutes that we looked upon the corpses all about us gave a picture that has always been as distinct as one before my very eyes.

So thick were the bodies of the dead that we had to step over them to get [near] a man in whom there was still life. Close to my feet was a young man who had been shot through the forehead. He had dropped dead with his eyes staring wildly open and, as he lay there, seemingly gazed up into my face.

I remember seeing poor old Colonel Davy Crockett as he lay dead by the side of a dying man, whose bloody and powder-stained face I was washing. Colonel Crockett was about fifty years old at that time. His coat and rough woolen shirt were soaked with blood so that the original color was hidden, for the eccentric hero must have died of some ball in the chest or a bayonet thrust.

15

EL MOSQUITO MEXICANO

Article Criticizing U.S. Interests in Texas

June 14, 1836

Throughout the early nineteenth century, Mexico's press viewed the actions of the United States with suspicion. This attitude was evident in the Mexico City newspaper El Mosquito Mexicano. *Notice the article's criticism of both the United States and Mexico.*

El Mosquito Mexicano, June 14, 1836, 1–2. Translated by Ernesto Chávez.

It would be most pleasing if the supreme government could achieve the nation's vengeance for the insults that have been waged against it and that it has suffered from that corrupt and aggressive part of North America. They say that the government has abundant resources to wage a war that would not be, in our estimation, only against a gang of thieves, namely the [Texas] colonists, but would instead have to be against the entire Northern nation [the United States]. This fact we deduce by observing the manner by which that government, as well as its judicial power, has conducted itself with respect to the Texas insurrection. Although it has tried to hide its sympathies with the weak mask of scandalous hypocrisy, one can deduce its stance by observing the persistence of that [C]ongress in supporting the independence of Texas, which leads us to declare that that government would raise troops and join in the consummation of an unjust and scandalous robbery. And who does not see in the deliberations of the [C]ongress that that approval is equivalent to permitting President Jackson to make war with Mexico, not clandestinely, but openly, trampling, with an absolute lack of modesty, the solemn pact that that nation celebrated with Mexico and which in the end has been reduced to fraud.

But the question among Mexicans is whether or not the government has the positive resources for such a war, and whether these resources would be able to compete with those of the North. We think that no one will lament the fact that we discuss this very important matter frankly, and we also believe that it is not a crime to emit our opinion with a healthy desire to prevent the immense evils that threaten the republic, and that will come to bear, if she, at this hour, does not return from that lethargy that we all see that her public spirit now finds herself in.

16

DANIEL WEBSTER

The Admission of Texas

December 22, 1845

Massachusetts senator Daniel Webster conveyed his concerns about the Lone Star Republic's admission into the Union in this speech delivered in the U.S. Senate on December 22, 1845, after Texas had formally accepted the United States' offer of annexation.

I am quite aware, Mr. President, that this resolution will pass the Senate. It has passed the other house of Congress by a large majority, and it is quite well known that there is a decided majority in this house also in favor of its passage. There are members of this body, Sir, who opposed the measures for the annexation of Texas which came before Congress at its last session, who, nevertheless, will very probably feel themselves now, in consequence of the resolutions of the last session, and in consequence of the proceedings of Texas upon those resolutions, bound to vote for her admission into the Union. I do not intend, Mr. President, to argue either of the questions which were discussed in Congress at that time, and which have been so much discussed throughout the country within the last three years.

Mr. President, there is no citizen of this country who has been more kindly disposed towards the people of Texas than myself, from the time they achieved, in so very extraordinary a manner, their independence of the Mexican government. I have shown, I hope, in another place, and shall show in all situations, and under all circumstances, a just and proper regard for the people of that country; but with respect to its annexation to this Union it is well known that, from the first announcement of any such idea, I have felt it my duty steadily, uniformly, and zealously to oppose it. I have expressed opinions and urged arguments against it everywhere, and on all occasions on which the subject came under consideration. I could not now, if I were to go

---

From Daniel Webster, *The Writings and Speeches of Daniel Webster* (Boston: Little, Brown, 1903), 9:54–59.

over the whole topic again, adduce any new views, or support old views, as far as I am aware, by any new arguments or illustrations. My efforts have been constant and unwearied; but, like those of others in the same cause, they have failed of success. I will therefore, Sir, in very few words, acting under the unanimous resolution and instructions of both branches of the legislature of Massachusetts, as well as in conformity to my own settled judgment and full conviction, recapitulate before the Senate and before the community the objections which have prevailed, and must always prevail, with me against this measure of annexation.

In the first place, I have, on the deepest reflection, long ago come to the conclusion, that it is of very dangerous tendency and doubtful consequences to enlarge the boundaries of this country, or the territories over which our laws are now established. There must be some limit to the extent of our territory, if we would make our institutions permanent. And this permanency forms the great subject of all my political efforts, the paramount object of my political regard. The government is very likely to be endangered, in my opinion, by a further enlargement of the territorial surface, already so vast, over which it is extended.

In the next place, I have always wished that this country should exhibit to the nations of the earth the example of a great, rich, and powerful republic, which is not possessed by a spirit of aggrandizement. It is an example, I think, due from us to the world, in favor of the character of republican government.

In the next place, Sir, I have to say, that while I hold, with as much integrity, I trust, and faithfulness, as any citizen of this country, to all the original arrangements and compromises under which the Constitution under which we now live was adopted, I never could, and never can, persuade myself to be in favor of the admission of other States into the Union as slave States, with the inequalities which were allowed and accorded by the Constitution to the slave-holding States then in existence. I do not think that the free States ever expected, or could expect, that they would be called on to admit more slave States, having the unequal advantages arising to them from the mode of apportioning representation under the existing Constitution.

17

JOHN SLIDELL

Diplomatic Dispatches to James Buchanan

January 1846

---

*Along with settling the Texas boundary dispute and claims of American
merchants against the Mexican government, John Slidell, "envoy extraordinaire and minister plenipotentiary," was also secretly charged with
securing New Mexico and California for the United States. His dispatches from Mexico to Secretary of State James Buchanan detailed his
dealings with the Mexican government and the upheaval there.*

No. 7

MEXICO, JANUARY 14, 1846.

SIR: . . . The contest between the military and the Government termi-
nated as I had expected. On the night of the 29 December, the greater
portion of the troops in garrison here pronounced in favor of the revolutionists, one regiment only, that stationed in the Palace, preserved a
semblance of fidelity, but it was well known that many of its officers
were disaffected, and on the following day, General Herrera, satisfied
that he could make no effectual resistance, resigned the Presidency.
The ringing of bells, and firing of cannon, announced the success of
the revolutionists, and the overthrow of the Government. When it is
recollected that the civil authorities throughout the country, with the
single exception of San Luis de Potosi, were opposed to the movement
of [General Mariano] Paredes, that most of them had made loud
protestations of their intention to resist it at all hazards, that both
branches of Congress had unanimously declared their abhorrence of
his treachery, and denounced his plan as an undisguised military despotism, and that, after all this war of manifestoes and resolutions, not a
shot has been fired in defence of the Constitutional Government, you
may form some idea of the utter imbecility of the people, and of the

---

From William Manning, ed., *Diplomatic Correspondence of the United States: Inter-Amer-
ican Affairs, 1831–1861 (Washington, D.C.: Carnegie Endowment for International
Peace, 1937), 8:808–10.

uncontrolled supremacy exercised by the army, in this miscalled Republic.

On the resignation of Herrera, General Valencia, one of the revolutionists, who as President of the council of Government, by the then existing constitution, became President ad interim of the Republic, assumed to act in that capacity, and it is said, during his brief exercise of power, converted to his own use, the greater share of the money which was found in the Treasury, his conduct on previous occasions justifies the belief that the charge is not without foundation. He affected regal state, being accompanied in all his movements, by a numerous and brilliant escort, his reign however was but a short one, even for this land of mushroom greatness. He invited Paredes to a conference in the city, which was declined, in the mean time the troops here, whom he had instigated to revolt, declared their preference for Paredes, the [he?] then, with Almonte, Tornel & other leaders of the revolution, proceeded to the headquarters of Paredes, where they were given by him to understand that having the army in his favor, he intended to organize a new government in his own way. The President ad interim was received with great hauteur. [I]t is understood indeed that he was apostrophized[1] by Paredes in terms of unmeasured reproach, and contempt. On the 2 January, Paredes entered the capital with his troops, those already stationed here, joining his triumphal march. On the same day, a junta of military officers, convened by him, met and established a plan of provisional government, to be administered by a President elected by a body composed of two notables from each department, these notables nominated by Paredes, met on the following evening, and, as you may readily imagine, unanimously elected him President, and on the 4 instant,[2] he took the oath of office. . . .

Whatever may be the fate of Paredes, I feel assured that no stable republican Government can be established in Mexico. The materials do not exist to constitute a people capable of self government. She is doomed for many years, to be the prey of conflicting factions, revolution is not an exceptional, but her normal state. She must soon cease to exercise any control over the remoter Departments. Yucatan is already virtually ind[e]pendent, Tabasco will soon be in the same situation, the allegiance of California is almost nominal, while New Mexico, Chihuahua, and Durango, exposed without protection to the

[1]*apostrophized*: A digression that pointedly addresses a person.
[2]*instant*: The current month.

incursions of the neighbouring savage tribes, will gladly seize on the first favorable occasion to free themselves from a connection, attended with manifold oppressions and burdens, and from which they can never by possibility derive any advantage. A war with the United States would be the signal for a general insurrection in those Departments. . . .

I send the letter of Mr. Peña y Peña[3] addressed to you, which being sealed, I declined forwarding until furnished with a copy. I have taken the liberty of breaking the seal, you will find the letter to be a brief summary of his note to me of 20 December.

No. 8

JALAPA, *February 6, 1846.*

SIR: I reached this place on the 20th ultimo.[4] Since my despatch of 14th ultimo, nothing has occurred to indicate the course likely to be taken by the existing Government as to my reception, but I think that it will mainly be controlled by the aspect of the Oregon question. Should our difficulties with Great Britain continue to present a prospect of war with that power, there will be but a very faint hope of a change of policy here. If on the contrary, negotiations be renewed with England, and there be a reasonable expectation of an amicable arrangement, I believe that pretexts will not be wanting for a reconsideration of the decision of the Herrera cabinet— I send you a copy of a communication of Mr. Peña y Peña to the Council of Government, made on the 11th December, inviting an expression of the opinion of the Council on the subject of my recognition, and suggesting his reasons why it should be refused. This document presents in the most glaring light, the bad faith of the late Government, and, in connection with the statement of Consul Black[5] accompanying my dispatch of 17th December, sh[o]ws in the most conclusive manner, that from the moment my arrival was announced, it had determined to avail itself of any pretence however frivolous, to refuse a reception, in the hope that by thus depriving its opponents of their chief theme of reproach and agitation, the impending blow would be averted— Mr. Peña y Peña after stating to the Council, substantially, the same objections to my credentials as are embodied in his note to me of 20th December, gives

---

[3]Manuel de la Peña y Peña, Minister of Foreign Relations.
[4]*ultimo*: Literally last, but in this case it means the previous month (January).
[5]John Black, U.S. consul in Veracruz.

as an additional and conclusive reason for their insufficiency, the fact of my appointment not having been confirmed by the Senate— It is a paper which presents in strong relief, the characteristic features of Mexican statesmanship, chicanery and ignorance, and will aid you in forming a more correct idea of the men who control the destinies of this unhappy country—

18

GENERAL PEDRO DE AMPUDIA
AND GENERAL ZACHARY TAYLOR

Dispatches

April 12, 1846

Written after U.S. forces were sent to the area between the Nueces River and the Rio Grande (called the Rio Bravo del Norte by the Mexicans) and before actual fighting began, this correspondence between Mexican commander Pedro de Ampudia and U.S. general Zachary Taylor sheds light on the tensions there.

General Pedro de Ampudia

HEADQUARTERS AT MATAMORAS, 2 O'CLOCK P.M.,
GOD AND LIBERTY!

APRIL 12, 1846.

Fourth Military Division, General-in-Chief:
   To explain to you the many grounds for the just grievances felt by the Mexican nation, caused by the United States government, would be a loss of time, and an insult to your good sense; I therefore pass at once to such explanations as I consider of absolute necessity.
   Your government, in an incredible manner—you will even permit me to say an extravagant one, if the [usage] or general rules estab-

From *A Brilliant National Record: General Taylor's Life, Battles, and Dispatches* (Philadelphia: T. C. Clarke, 1847), 43.

lished and received among all civilized nations are regarded—has not only insulted, but has exasperated the Mexican nation, bearing its conquering banner to the left bank of the Rio Bravo del Norte; and in this case, by explicit and definitive orders of my government, which neither can, will, nor should receive new outrages, I require you in all form, and at latest in the peremptory term of twenty-four hours, to break up your camp and retire to the other bank of the Nueces river while our governments are regulating the pending question in relation to Texas. If you insist in remaining upon the soil of the department of Tamaulipas, it will clearly result that arms, and arms alone, must decide the question; and in that case I advise you that we accept the war to which, with so much injustice on your part you provoke us, and that, on our part, this war shall be conducted conformably to the principles established by the most civilized nations; that is to say, that the law of nations and of war shall be the guide of my operations; trusting that on your part the same will be observed.

With this view, I tender you the considerations due to your person and respectable office.

PEDRO DE AMPUDIA.

Senor General-in-Chief of the U.S. Army, Don Z. TAYLOR.

General Zachary Taylor

HEADQUARTERS, ARMY OF OCCUPATION.

Camp near Matamoras, Texas, April 12, 1846.

Senor:

I have had the honor to receive your note of this date, in which you summon me to withdraw the forces under my command from their present position, and beyond the river Nueces, until the pending question between our governments, relative to the limits of Texas, shall be settled.

I need hardly advise you that, charged as I am, in only a military capacity, with the performance of specific duties, I cannot enter into a discussion of the international question involved in the advance of the American army. You will, however, permit me to say that the government of the United States has constantly sought a settlement, by negotiation, of the question of boundary; that as envoy was despatched to Mexico for that purpose, and that up to the most recent dates said envoy had not been received by the actual Mexican government, if indeed he has not received his passports and left the republic. In the mean time, I have been ordered to occupy the country up to the left bank of the Rio Grande, until the boundary shall be definitely settled. In carrying out these instructions I have carefully abstained from all sets of hostility, obeying in this regard, not only the letter of my instructions, but the plain dictates of justice and humanity.

The instructions under which I am acting will not permit me to retrograde[1] from the position I now occupy. In view of the relations between our respective governments, and the individual suffering which may result, I regret the alternative which you offer; but, at the same time, wish it understood that I shall by no means avoid such alternative, leaving the responsibility with those who rashly commence hostilities. In conclusion, you will permit me to give the assurance that on my part the laws and customs of war among civilized nations shall be carefully observed.

I have the honor to be, very respectfully, your obedient servant.

Z. TAYLOR.

Senor General D. PEDRO DE AMPUDIA.

[1] *retrograde*: Turn back.

19

GENERAL ZACHARY TAYLOR

Dispatch to Adjutant General of the Army

April 26, 1846

General Taylor sent this dispatch to the adjutant general of the U.S. Army following the skirmish at Rancho de Carricitos, located between the Nueces River and the Rio Grande. Note how Taylor described the situation, and compare it to President James K. Polk's depiction of the event (Document 20).

From Ward McAfee and J. Cordell Robinson, eds., *Origins of the Mexican War: A Documentary Source Book* (Salisbury, N.C.: Documentary Publications, 1982), 2:137.

ZACHARY TAYLOR, Brigadier General Commanding United States Army in
Texas, to Adjutant General of the Army

Camp opposite Matamoros, April 26, 1846

I have respectfully to report that General Arista arrived in Matamoros
on the 24th instant and assumed the chief command of the Mexican
troops. On the same day he addressed me a communication, conceived in courteous terms, but saying that he considered hostilities
commenced, and should prosecute them. A translation of his note and
copy of my reply will be transmitted the moment they can be prepared. I dispatch this by an express which is now waiting.

I regret to report that a party of dragoons sent out by me on the
24th instant to watch the course of the river above on this bank
became engaged with a very large force of the enemy, and after a
short affair in which some sixteen were killed and wounded, [the
party] appears to have been surrounded and compelled to surrender.
Not one of the party has returned, except a wounded man sent in this
morning by the Mexican commander, so that I cannot report with confidence the particulars of the engagement or the fate of the officers,
except that Capt. Hardee was known to be a prisoner and unhurt.
Capt. Thornton and Lieutenants Mason and Kane were the other officers. The party was 63 strong.

Hostilities may now be considered as commenced, and I have this
day deemed it necessary to call upon the governor of Texas for four
regiments of volunteers, two to be mounted and two to serve on foot.
As some delay must occur in collecting these troops, I have also
desired the governor of Louisiana to send out four regiments of
infantry as soon as practicable. This will constitute an auxiliary force
of nearly 5,000 men, which will be required to prosecute the war with
energy, and carry it, as it should be, into the enemy's country. I trust
the department will approve my course in this matter and will give the
necessary orders to the staff departments for the supply of this large
additional force.

If a law could be passed authorizing the President to raise volunteers for 12 months, it would be of the greatest importance for a
service so remote from support as this.

20

PRESIDENT JAMES K. POLK

War Message to Congress

May, 11, 1846

President Polk wrote this message in the style of a legal brief in an effort to convince Congress of the need for war with Mexico. Although he began writing it before the events between the Nueces River and the Rio Grande occurred, the military hostilities there served as the final piece of evidence the president needed to justify his condemnation of Mexico.

WASHINGTON, *May 11, 1846.*

To the Senate and House of Representatives:

The existing state of the relations between the United States and Mexico renders it proper that I should bring the subject to the consideration of Congress. In my message at the commencement of your present session the state of these relations, the causes which led to the suspension of diplomatic intercourse between the two countries in March, 1845, and the long-continued and unredressed wrongs and injuries committed by the Mexican Government on citizens of the United States in their persons and property were briefly set forth.

As the facts and opinions which were then laid before you were carefully considered, I can not better express my present convictions of the condition of affairs up to that time than by referring you to that communication.

The strong desire to establish peace with Mexico on liberal and honorable terms, and the readiness of this Government to regulate and adjust our boundary and other causes of difference with that power on such fair and equitable principles as would lead to permanent relations of the most friendly nature, induced me in September last to seek the reopening of diplomatic relations between the two countries. Every measure adopted on our part had for its object the

---

From James Richardson, ed., *A Compilation of the Messages and Papers of the Presidents of the United States, 1789–1897* (Washington, D.C.: Government Printing Office, 1897), 4:437–38, 441–42.

furtherance of these desired results. In communicating to Congress a succinct statement of the injuries which we had suffered from Mexico, and which have been accumulating during a period of more than twenty years, every expression that could tend to inflame the people of Mexico or defeat or delay a pacific result was carefully avoided. An envoy of the United States repaired to Mexico with full powers to adjust every existing difference. But though present on the Mexican soil by agreement between the two Governments, invested with full powers, and bearing evidence of the most friendly dispositions, his mission has been unavailing. The Mexican Government not only refused to receive him or listen to his propositions, but after a long-continued series of menaces have at last invaded our territory and shed the blood of our fellow-citizens on our own soil. . . .

The movement of the troops to the Del Norte was made by the commanding general under positive instructions to abstain from all aggressive acts toward Mexico or Mexican citizens and to regard the relations between that Republic and the United States as peaceful unless she should declare war or commit acts of hostility indicative of a state of war. He was specially directed to protect private property and respect personal rights.

The Army moved from Corpus Christi on the 11th of March, and on the 28th of that month arrived on the left bank of the Del Norte opposite to Matamoras, where it encamped on a commanding position, which has since been strengthened by the erection of fieldworks. A depot has also been established at Point Isabel, near the Brazos Santiago, 30 miles in rear of the encampment. The selection of his position was necessarily confided to the judgment of the general in command.

The Mexican forces at Matamoras assumed a belligerent attitude, and on the 12th of April General Ampudia, then in command, notified General Taylor to break up his camp within twenty-four hours and to retire beyond the Nueces River, and in the event of his failure to comply with these demands announced that arms, and arms alone, must decide the question. But no open act of hostility was committed until the 24th of April. On that day General Arista, who had succeeded to the command of the Mexican forces, communicated to General Taylor that "he considered hostilities commenced and should prosecute them." A party of dragoons of 63 men and officers were on the same day dispatched from the American camp up the Rio del Norte, on its left bank, to ascertain whether the Mexican troops had crossed or were preparing to cross the river, "became engaged with a large body of these troops, and after a short affair, in which some 16 were killed and wounded, appear to have been surrounded and compelled to surrender."

The grievous wrongs perpetrated by Mexico upon our citizens throughout a long period of years remain unredressed, and solemn treaties pledging her public faith for this redress have been disregarded. A government either unable or unwilling to enforce the execution of such treaties fails to perform one of its plainest duties. . . .

Our commerce with Mexico has been almost annihilated. It was formerly highly beneficial to both nations, but our merchants have been deterred from prosecuting it by the system of outrage and extortion which the Mexican authorities have pursued against them, whilst their appeals through their own Government for indemnity have been made in vain. Our forbearance has gone to such an extreme as to be mistaken in its character. Had we acted with vigor in repelling the insults and redressing the injuries inflicted by Mexico at the commencement, we should doubtless have escaped all the difficulties in which we are now involved.

Instead of this, however, we have been exerting our best efforts to propitiate her good will. Upon the pretext that Texas, a nation as independent as herself, thought proper to unite its destinies with our own, she has affected to believe that we have severed her rightful territory, and in official proclamations and manifestoes has repeatedly threatened to make war upon us for the purpose of reconquering Texas. In the meantime we have tried every effort at reconciliation. The cup of forbearance had been exhausted even before the recent information from the frontier of the Del Norte. But now, after reiterated menaces, Mexico has passed the boundary of the United States, has invaded our territory and shed American blood upon the American soil. She has proclaimed that hostilities have commenced, and that the two nations are now at war.

As war exists, and, notwithstanding all our efforts to avoid it, exists by the act of Mexico herself, we are called upon by every consideration of duty and patriotism to vindicate with decision the honor, the rights, and the interests of our country.

21

HUGH WHITE

Statement against the Two-Million-Dollar Bill
August 8, 1846

Hugh White, a Whig congressman from New York, was the first member of the House of Representatives to link the war with slavery.

Within the time allowed me, . . . I desire to state that it is my intention to publish some remarks which I intended to have made upon this Mexican war — a war, in my judgment, unnecessary, uncalled for, and wholly unjustifiable; offensive in its inception, and I fear of conquest and subjugation in its ending. The President, in his message to this House, on the 11th of May last, has furnished abundant evidence that this war was projected, planned, and provoked long before any counsel or assistance was asked or required from Congress. It was the act of the President himself, and he has furnished the proof in that document; yet this House furnished him with ample means to conduct and carry on hostilities; fifty thousand men and thirty millions of money were promptly voted to sustain him in this undertaking, which all good men must consider as unjust, inglorious, and wicked; but, inasmuch as hostilities existed, and our army was in imminent peril, the causes were overlooked, and consequences left to their course. And now, sir, we come to the subject before us — the message of the President and the bill appropriating, as recommended by that message, two millions of dollars; and for what purpose? Why, sir, to buy a peace. Is that true? Has not the President ample power to conclude a peace with Mexico if she demands or desires one? Is the mode of warfare to be changed from fighting to purchasing? Who is to be bought? And what evidence have we that anybody or thing is purchasable? Is this to be a corruption fund in the hands of the President, to use at his pleasure and discretion? Sir, I have no confidence in this application. We have no evidence before us of its necessity, no information of its use or application; we are in the dark, and required to vote in the dark, or be

From *Congressional Globe*, 29th Cong., 1st sess., 1846, 1213–1214.

charged with opposing measures of peace. If there is the slightest prospect of peace, any glimmer or faint ray of that heavenly messenger, why could it not have been communicated to this House. I repeat, sir, I have no confidence in this application for money; territory is what is sought after, and I cannot give my sanction to this appropriation, unless the bill now upon your table shall be so amended as to forever preclude the possibility of extending the limits of slavery. And I call upon gentlemen on the other side of the House to bring forward such amendments as shall effectually prevent the further acquisition of territory, which may be caused by the adoption of that institution. I call upon the other side of the House to propose such an amendment, not only as an evidence of their desire to restrain that institution within its constitutional limits, but as a guaranty that the President will honestly and faithfully apply the funds so generously placed in his hands to the ends specified in his message.

22

DAVID WILMOT

Wilmot Proviso

August 8, 1846

Following President Polk's request to Congress for the "Two-Million-Dollar Bill," Democratic congressman David Wilmot of Pennsylvania presented this antislavery provision to the legislation. The proviso originated with Representative Jacob Brinkerhoff of Ohio, but Wilmot was asked to introduce the bill because of his prominent standing in the party. The proviso passed in the House of Representatives but was tabled in the Senate. Nonetheless, it ensured the bill's defeat, as well as the defeat of any other appropriation bills to which a similar proviso was attached. Note the proviso's wording and think about other legislation in U.S. history that used similar language.

From Archie P. McDonald, *The Mexican War: Crisis of American Democracy* (Lexington, Mass.: D. C. Heath, 1966), 40.

Provided, That, as an express and fundamental condition to the acquisition of any territory from the Republic of Mexico by the United
States, by virtue of any treaty which may be negotiated between them,
and to the use by the Executive of the moneys herein appropriated,
neither slavery nor involuntary servitude shall ever exist in any part
of said territory, except for crime, whereof the party shall first be duly
convicted.

23

FREDERICK DOUGLASS

The War with Mexico

January 21, 1848

*Frederick Douglass was perhaps the most widely known African Ameri-
can of his time. Born into slavery in 1817, Douglass educated himself,
eventually bought his freedom, and became a vocal opponent of slavery.
Published toward the end of the war in his newspaper, the* North Star,
*Douglass's condemnation expressed many African Americans' views of
the conflict. For Douglass, as for other African Americans, the war had
personal significance. Compare Douglass's view of Mexico and Mexicans
with the views of other people writing during this period, including Walt
Whitman, Susan Shelby Magoffin, and John Slidell.*

We have no preference for parties, regarding this slaveholding crusade.
The one is as bad as the other. The friends of peace have nothing to
hope from either. The Democrats claim the credit of commencing, and
the Whigs monopolize the glory of voting supplies and carrying on
the war; branding the war as dishonorably commenced, yet boldly per-
sisting in pressing it on. If we have any preference of two such parties,
that preference inclines to the one whose practice, though wicked,

From Frederick Douglass, "The War with Mexico," *North Star*, January 21, 1848, 2.
Reprinted from Phillip S. Foner, ed., *The Life and Writings of Frederick Douglass, Early
Years, 1817–1849* (New York: International Publishers, 1950), 293–95.

most accords with its professions. We know where to find the so called Democrats. They are the accustomed panderers to slaveholders: nothing is either too mean, too dirty, or infamous for them, when commanded by the merciless man stealers of our country. No one expects any thing honorable or decent from that party, touching human rights. They annexed Texas under the plea of extending the area of freedom. They elected James K. Polk, the slaveholder, as the friend of freedom; and they have backed him up in his Presidential falsehoods. They have used their utmost endeavors to crush the right of speech, abridge the right of petition, and to perpetuate the enslavement of the colored people of this country. But we do not intend to go into any examination of parties just now. That we shall have frequent opportunities of doing hereafter. We wish merely to give our readers a general portrait of the present aspect of our country in regard to the Mexican war, its designs, and its results, as they have thus far transpired. . . .

In watching the effects of the war spirit, prominent among them, will be seen, not only the subversion of the great principles of Christian morality, but the most horrid blasphemy.

While traveling from Rochester to Victor, [New York,] a few days ago, we listened to a conversation between two persons of apparent gentility and intelligence, on the subject of the United States' war against Mexico. A wide difference of opinion appeared between them; the one contending for the rightfulness of the war, and the other against it. The main argument in favor of the war was the meanness and wickedness of the Mexican people; and, to cap the climax, he gave it as his solemn conviction, that the hand of the Lord was in the work! That the cup of Mexican iniquity was full; and that God was now making use of the Anglo Saxon race as a rod to chastise them! The effect of this religious outburst was to stun his opponent into silence: he seemed speechless; the ground was too high and holy for him; he did not dare reply to it; and thus the conversation ended. When men charge their sins upon God, argument is idle; rebuke alone is needful; and the poor man, lacking the moral courage to do this, sat silent.

Here, then, we have religion coupled with our murderous designs. We are, in the hands of the great God, a rod to chastise this rebellious people! What say our evangelical clergy to this blasphemy? That clergy seem as silent as the grave; and their silence is the greatest sanction of the crime. They have seen the blood of the innocent poured out like water, and are dumb; they have seen the truth trampled in the dust—right sought by pursuing the wrong—peace sought by prosecuting the war—honor sought by dishonorable means—and have not raised a whisper against it: they float down with the multitude in the filthy current of crime, and are hand in hand with the guilty. Had the pulpit been faithful, we might have been saved from this withering curse. We sometimes fear, that now our case as a nation is hopeless. May God grant otherwise! Our nation seems resolved to rush on in her wicked career, though the road be ditched with human blood, and paved with human skulls. Well, be it so. But, humble as we are, and unavailing as our voice may be, we wish to warn our fellow countrymen, that they may follow the course which they have marked out for themselves; no barrier may be sufficient to obstruct them; they may accomplish all they desire; Mexico may fall before them; she may be conquered and subdued; her government may be annihilated—her name among the great sisterhood of nations blotted out; her separate existence annihilated; her rights and powers usurped; her people put under the iron arm of a military despotism, and reduced to a condition little better than that endured by the Saxons when vanquished by their Norman invaders; but, so sure as there is a God of justice, we shall not go unpunished.

24

NEW YORK HERALD

Editorial in Support of the War with Mexico
February 20, 1847

The New York Herald's *founder, publisher, and editor, James Gordon Bennett, supported the Democratic Party, and thus his newspaper espoused pro-war views. The* Herald *reported on rallies in support of the war and ran articles calling for continued fighting throughout the war. Note how Mexico is described and think about how this depiction might have influenced readers to support the war.*

From "The Great War Meeting—Its Aspect and Importance," editorial, *New York Herald*, February 20, 1847, 2.

If there had been a doubt in the mind of any person that the masses of the people were divided in opinion on the propriety of supporting the administration, and furnishing them with men and means to bring the war with Mexico to an honorable and victorious conclusion, and as speedily as possible, the enthusiasm that was manifested at the great war meeting in this city, on Thursday evening last, was calculated to dissipate it. We have attended many popular meetings in our time, but we never saw at any, a more decided, determined, and unanimous expression of the popular will. There was, to be sure, a covert attempt made by certain parties, to throw a firebrand into the vast assembly, but the moment it was discovered, it was quenched.

The next question is, what effect will this meeting, and the pointed and pungent resolutions that were so unanimously carried with three times three cheers, have on the factious disorganizers in and out of Congress? . . .

Will this severe and well-merited rebuke, administered to them by the people. . . , have the effect of making them pause in their factious and headlong career, and induce them to make reparation to their injured country for the wrongs they have wilfully inflicted on her, and the stigma they have cast on our flag?

We hope, for the honor of our country, it will. We hope, for our reputation as a republican people that it will. But if it do not, we pity the man or set of men, who will dare to beard[1] the people, and defy the solemnly and determinedly expressed will of their constituents. If it do not, the contract that they entered into with their constituents is at an end. The relation they assumed when they accepted their nominations—a relation of agent[s] to carry out the will of their constituents—will be at an end, and then resignation should follow.

The people insist that this war shall be prosecuted with vigor— they have given their unworthy representatives to understand that they were elected to carry out the views of their constituents, and not occupy their time, which is so precious, in the present emergency, in debating whether slavery, shall have a foothold in the moon; for they might as well discuss its existence there, as in the new territory that we may acquire. They have spoken in thunder tones to those who use their brief power for the furtherance of their own factious and selfish views.

---

[1] *beard*: To oppose boldly or defy.

We hope that similar meetings to that held here, will be held all over the country, and if other cities and towns utter such sentiments as those expressed at the meeting in New York, the death knell of political pettifogging[2] will be rung, and the glory and honor of the country be sustained and vindicated.

[2]*pettifogging*: Petty, shifty, or unethical practice.

25

WALT WHITMAN

War with Mexico

May 11, 1846

As editor of the Brooklyn Daily Eagle, *the poet and journalist Walt Whitman published several editorials supporting the war with Mexico. Although most of Whitman's pieces had a confrontational tone, they became less zealous as the conflict wore on. By January 1847, he believed that Mexico had been punished enough and appealed for an end to the war. Notice Whitman's racialized views of Mexicans.*

Yes: Mexico must be thoroughly chastised!—We have reached a point in our intercourse with that country, when prompt and effectual demonstrations of force are enjoined upon us by every dictate of right and policy. The news of yesterday has added the last argument wanted to prove the necessity of an immediate Declaration of War by our government toward its southern neighbor.

We are justified in the face of the world, in having treated Mexico with more forbearance than we have ever yet treated an enemy—for Mexico, though contemptible in many respects, is an enemy deserv-

From Walt Whitman, *The Gathering of the Forces: Editorials, Essays, Literary and Dramatic Reviews and Other Material Written by Walt Whitman as Editor of the Brooklyn Daily Eagle in 1846 and 1847*, ed. Cleveland Rodgers and John Black (New York: G. P. Putnam's Sons, 1920), 240–42, 246–47.

ing a vigorous "lesson." We have coaxed, excused, listened with deaf ears to the insolent gasconnade[1] of her government, submitted thus far to a most offensive rejection of an Ambassador personifying the American nation, and waited for years without payment of the claims of our injured merchants. We have sought peace through every avenue, and shut our eyes to many things, which had they come from England or France, the President would not have dared to pass over without stern and speedy resentment. We have dammed up our memory, of what has passed in the South years ago—of the devilish massacres of some of our bravest and noblest sons, the children not of the South alone, but of the North and West—massacres, not only in defiance of ordinary humanity, but in violation of all the rules of war. Who has read the sickening story of those brutal wholesale murders, so useless for any purpose except gratifying the cowardly appetite of a nation of bravos,[2] willing to shoot down men by the hundred in cold blood—without panting for the day when the prayer of that blood should be listened to—when the vengeance of a retributive God should be meted out to those who so ruthlessly and needlessly slaughtered His image?

That day has arrived. We think there can be no doubt of the truth of yesterday's news; and we are sure the people here, ten to one, are for prompt and *effectual* hostilities. Tame newspaper comments, such as appear in the leading Democratic print of today, in New York, and the contemptible anti-patriotic criticism of its contemporary Whig organ, do *not* express the sentiments and wishes of *the people*. Let our arms now be carried with a spirit which shall teach the world that, while we are not forward for a quarrel, America knows how to crush, as well as how to expand!

---

[1] *gasconnade*: Extravagant boasting.
[2] *bravos*: Daring bandits or assassins.

26

THEODORE PARKER

A Sermon of the Mexican War

June 1846

The Congregational minister, abolitionist, transcendentalist, and peace advocate Theodore Parker denounced the conflict in Mexico in this sermon delivered at an antiwar meeting in Boston in June 1846. Parker was highly influential among antiwar critics, counted Ralph Waldo Emerson and Henry David Thoreau among his friends, and maintained a correspondence with Lieutenant Colonel Ethan Allen Hitchcock, an aide to General Winfield Scott who believed that the conflict was a mistake. Notice Parker's reasons for his denunciation of the war.

But why talk for ever? What shall we do? In regard to this present war, we can refuse to take any part in it; we can encourage others to do the same; we can aid men, if need be, who suffer because they refuse. Men will call us traitors: what then? That hurt nobody in '76! We are a rebellious nation; our whole history is treason; our blood was at-tainted[1] before we were born; our creeds are infidelity to the mother-church; our Constitution treason to our fatherland. What of that? Though all the governors in the world bid us commit treason against man, and set the example, let us never submit. Let God only be a master to control our conscience!

We can hold public meetings in favour of peace, in which what is wrong shall be exposed and condemned. It is proof of our cowardice that this has not been done before now. We can show in what the infamy of a nation consists; in what its real glory. One of your own men, the last summer, startled the churches out of their sleep, by his manly trumpet, talking with us, and telling that the true grandeur of a nation was justice, not glory; peace, not war.

---

[1] *attainted*: Corrupted.

From Frances P. Cobbe, ed., *Sermons on War, Comprising A Sermon of War, Speech Delivered at the Anti-War Meeting. A Sermon of the Mexican War, from the Collected Works of Theodore Parker* (New York: Garland, 1973), 27–29.

We can work now for future times, by taking pains to spread abroad the sentiments of peace, the ideas of peace, among the people in schools, churches—everywhere. At length we can diminish the power of the national Government, so that the people alone shall have the power to declare war, by a direct vote, the Congress only to recommend it. We can take from the Government the means of war, by raising only revenue enough for the nation's actual wants, and raising that directly, so that each man knows what he pays, and when he pays it, and then he will take care that it is not paid to make him poor and keep him so. We can diffuse a real practical Christianity among the people, till the mass of men have courage enough to overcome evil with good, and look at aggressive war as the worst of treason and the foulest infidelity!

Now is the time to push and be active. War itself gives weight to words of peace. There will never be a better time till we make the times better. It is not a day for cowardice, but for heroism. Fear not that the "honour of the nation" will suffer from Christian movements for peace. What if your men of low degree are a vanity, and your men of high degree are a lie? That is no new thing. Let true men do their duty, and the lie and the vanity will pass each to its reward. Wait not for the churches to move, or the State to become Christian. Let us bear our testimony like men, not fearing to be called traitors, infidels; fearing only to be such.

I would call on Americans, by their love of our country, its great ideas, its real grandeur, its hopes, and the memory of its fathers— to come and help to save that country from infamy and ruin. I would call on Christians, who believe that Christianity is a truth, to lift up their voice, public and private, against the foulest violation of God's law, this blasphemy of the Holy Spirit of Christ, this worst form of infidelity to man and God. I would call on all men, by the one nature that is in you, by the great human heart beating alike in all your bosoms, to protest manfully against this desecration of the earth, this high treason against both man and God. Teach your rulers that you are Americans, not slaves; Christians, not heathen; men, not murderers, to kill for hire! You may effect little in this generation, for its head seems crazed and its heart rotten. But there will be a day after today. It is for you and me to make it better: a day of peace, when nation shall no longer lift up sword against nation; when all shall indeed be brothers, and all blest. Do this, you shall be worthy to dwell in this beautiful land; Christ will be near you; God work with you, and bless you for ever!

27

HENRY DAVID THOREAU

On Civil Disobedience

1848

As a protest against the war with Mexico, the famous writer and philosopher Henry David Thoreau refused to pay his taxes in July 1846. Two years later, he published the essay "Resistance to Civil Government," originally a lecture, which appeared posthumously with the title "On Civil Disobedience." The piece inspired civil disobedience both in the United States and abroad and continues to serve as an inspiration to those who seek peaceful resistance to government policies.

I heartily accept the motto, "That government is best which governs least"; and I should like to see it acted up to more rapidly and systematically. Carried out, it finally amounts to this, which also I believe— "That government is best which governs not at all"; and when men are prepared for it, that will be the kind of government which they will have. Government is at best but an expedient; but most governments are usually, and all governments are sometimes, inexpedient. The objections which have been brought against a standing army, and they are many and weighty, and deserve to prevail, may also at last be brought against a standing government. The standing army is only an arm of the standing government. The government itself, which is only the mode which the people have chosen to execute their will, is equally liable to be abused and perverted before the people can act through it. Witness the present Mexican war, the work of comparatively a few individuals using the standing government as their tool; for, in the outset, the people would not have consented to this measure. . . .

But, to speak practically and as a citizen, unlike those who call themselves no-government men, I ask for, not at once no government, but *at once* a better government. Let every man make known what

---

From Henry David Thoreau, *Walden and Civil Disobedience*, ed. Paul Lauter (New York: Houghton Mifflin, 2000), 17–18, 20.

kind of government would command his respect, and that will be one step toward obtaining it. . . .

How does it become a man to behave toward this American government today? I answer, that he cannot without disgrace be associated with it. I cannot for an instant recognize that political organization as *my* government which is the *slave's* government also. . . .

Under a government which imprisons any unjustly, the true place for a just man is also a prison. The proper place today, the only place which Massachusetts has provided for her freer and less desponding spirits, is in her prisons, to be put out and locked out of the State by her own act, as they have already put themselves out by their principles. It is there that the fugitive slave, and the Mexican prisoner on parole, and the Indian come to plead the wrongs of his race should find them; on that separate, but more free and honorable, ground, where the State places those who are not *with* her, but *against* her— the only house in a slave State in which a free man can abide with honor. . . .

If a thousand men were not to pay their tax-bills this year, that would not be a violent and bloody measure, as it would be to pay them, and enable the State to commit violence and shed innocent blood.

This is, in fact, the definition of a peaceable revolution, if any such is possible. If the tax-gatherer, or any other public officer, asks me, as one has done, "But what shall I do?" my answer is, "If you really wish to do anything, resign your office." When the subject has refused allegiance, and the officer has resigned his office, then the revolution is accomplished. But even suppose blood should flow. Is there not a sort of blood shed when the conscience is wounded? Through this wound a man's real manhood and immortality flow out, and he bleeds to an everlasting death. I see this blood flowing now.

28

WOMEN OF EXETER, ENGLAND, AND PHILADELPHIA

Women's Peace Petition

June 1846

Because of the possibility of war between the United States and Great Britain, the American reformer Elihu Burritt solicited a letter from the women of Exeter, England, to the women of Philadelphia on the subject of peace. In it, 1,623 English women called on their American sisters to help prevent a conflict between their two countries. The Philadelphia women responded with a statement read by noted abolitionist and later women's rights advocate Lucretia Mott at a rally in their home city on June 17, 1846. Working within the confines of the cult of domesticity, these women believed it was in keeping with women's roles as mothers to influence society to move away from war and toward justice. Though inspired by the hostilities between Britain and the United States, the letter also applied to the war with Mexico.

THE FRIENDLY ADDRESS OF THE UNDERSIGNED WOMEN,
INHABITANTS OF THE CITY OF EXETER, IN ENGLAND, TO THE WOMEN
OF THE CITY OF PHILADELPHIA, AND OF THE UNITED STATES GENERALLY.

Beloved Friends and Sisters:

The suggestion of friendly international addresses, in order to deprecate war and create a pacific spirit, having been extensively approved and its adoption pressed upon all classes, we trust it will not be deemed unseemly in Women to seek, by the same means, to influence their American Sisters in the cause of Religion and Peace.

It may not be within our province to judge of the merits of the question now at issue between our respective governments, but we must all feel how greatly to be dreaded would be a resort to arms on any subject. Let us then, beloved Sisters, unite together, though separated by the mighty deep, in using the influence we possess, which is not

---

Pennsylvania Freeman, June 18, 1846, 2, and June 25, 1846, 3.

88

powerless though exerted chiefly around the domestic hearth: let us seek to infuse into the minds of our husbands, our fathers, our sons, and our brothers, and of all around us, a spirit of amity and concord, whispering peace where ever the sounds of discord are heard: and let us, as mothers, watch over the opening minds of our tender offspring, and point out to them that the way to true honor is not through fields of battle, but through the enlightened straightforward course of justice and equity prescribed by the Gospel of *"Peace on earth, and good will towards men."*

You and we have a common ancestry and are bound together by innumerable ties of consanguinity and mutual interest; surely then we ought to be united in the bonds of Christian love. How shall those whose interests require the maintenance of closest friendship, who ought to lose as brethren, meet on the field of battle to destroy each other!

Above all, let us unite in prayers to the Great Lord of the universe, who turneth the hearts of the children of men that he will dispose the rulers of both Countries to a pacific adjustment of their national differences, that so the reciprocal benefits of friendly intercourse may still be maintained, and that, under the benign influence of peace, the cause of Religion and Virtue may prosper, and these two great Nations perform their part in promoting the advance of that blissful period, foretold by the Prophet, when nation shall not lift up the sword against nation, and the people shall learn war no more.

With sentiments of sincere good will, we remain your Friends and Sisters,

RACHEL SPARKS, ELIZABETH KNOTT, MARLA SHEPPARD, and 1,620 others.

FROM THE WOMEN OF PHILADELPHIA, U.S.A., IN ANSWER TO THE FRIENDLY ADDRESS OF THE WOMEN OF EXETER, ENGLAND ON THE SUBJECT OF PEACE.

Dear Sisters:

Your Address has met with a cordial reception by us. Heartily do we respond to your earnest desire, that so terrible a calamity as war, between your country and ours, may never come upon us. We feel assured that the fraternal addresses sent by thousands of English men and women, will do much towards averting so fearful an evil. . . .

We hold it to be the duty of women, to look with an attentive eye upon the great events which are transpiring around them; in order that, with an enlightened judgment, as well as with a feeling heart, they may direct the force of their moral influence against the iniquitous spirit of war. Great is the responsibility of women, in relation to this subject. The false love of glory, the cruel spirit of revenge, the blood-thirsty ambition, swelling the breast of the soldier in the battle-field, these are often but the ripened harvest from the seed sown by his mother's hand, when in his childish hours she gave him tiny weapons, and taught him how to mimic war's murderous game.

Let us, dear sisters, be increasing faithful in all our relations, whether of the social circle, or the more extended sphere, by the mighty influences that cluster around the domestic hearth, and by the way side—by the pen and the press—in bearing testimony to the superiority of the law of Christian love and forgiveness, over that of physical force.

We are gratified that the present difficulties between our countries are being amicably settled; but let us not forget that we have other brethren, entitled to our sympathy, urging upon us the duty to impress upon the heart of this generation the idea of the brotherhood of the race. The war waged by your government in India, and that by ours against the Mexicans, admonish us that it is now, as ever, important to instil the principles of justice, mercy and peace.

For your word of counsel and cheer, we thank you: and would unite with you in prayer, that the kingdom of our Father in Heaven may come, and the gospel of his dear Son, breathing "peace on earth and good will to man, may extend from sea to sea, and from the river to the ends of the earth."

With reciprocal expressions of regard,
We are yours for universal Peace.

29

SUSAN SHELBY MAGOFFIN
Comments on Mexican Women
1846

Susan Shelby Magoffin was one of the first American women to travel into Mexican territory. Barely eighteen years old when she embarked on her journey in 1846, she accompanied her merchant husband, Samuel, down the Santa Fe Trail, through New Mexico and into Chihuahua. While on her travels, she kept a diary, noting the people and sights she saw and offering a distinct, and often racially biased, view of Mexican women. The Magoffins entered New Mexico two weeks after Mexican governor Manuel Armijo fled the capital, an act that facilitated the American occupation. Later, they followed Colonel Alexander Doniphan and his troops into Chihuahua.

Thursday 27. Near San Miguel. We have passed through some two or three little settlements today similar to the Vegas,[1] and I am glad to think that much is accomplished of my task. It is truly shocking to my modesty to pass such places with gentlemen.

The women slap about with their arms and necks bare, perhaps their bosoms exposed (and they are none of the prettiest or whitest) if they are about to cross the little creek that is near all the villages, regardless of those about them, they pull their dresses, which in the first place but little more than cover their calves—up above their knees and paddle through the water like ducks, sloshing and spattering every thing about them. Some of them wear leather shoes, from the States, but most have buckskin mockersins, Indian style.

And it is repulsive to see the children running about perfectly naked, or if they have on a chimese it is in such ribbands it had better

---

[1] *Vegas*: Las Vegas, New Mexico. Founded in 1835, it served as an important stop on the Santa Fe trail.

From Stella M. Drumm, ed., *Down the Santa Fe Trail and into Mexico: The Diary of Susan Shelby Magoffin, 1846–1847* (Lincoln: University of Nebraska Press, 1982), 95, 118–24.

be off at once. I am constrained to keep my veil drawn closely over my face all the time to protect my blushes. . . .

Friday 11th. What did I write of last yesterday? The managerie, well, now for a little critical view of it. I went in of course somewhat prepared to see; as I have often heard of such a show, I knew in a measure what to look for. First the ballroom, the walls of which were hung and fancifully decorated with the "stripes and stars," was opened to my view—there were before me numerous objects of the biped species, dressed in the seven rain-bow colours variously contrasted, and in fashions adapted to the reign of King Henry VIII, or of the great queen Elizabeth, *my memory* cannot exactly tell me which, they were entirely enveloped, on the first view in a cloud of smoke, and while some were circling in a mazy dance others were seated around the room next the wall enjoying the scene before them, and quietly puffing, both males and females their little cigarritas a delicate cigar made with a very little tobacco rolled in a corn shuck or bit of paper. I had not been seated more than fifteen minutes before Maj. Soards an officer, a man of quick perception, irony, sarcasm, and wit, came up to me in true Mexican style, and with a polite, "Madam will you have a cigarita," drew from one pocket a *handfull of shucks and from an other a large horn of tobacco*, at once turning the whole thing to a burlesque.

Among the officers of the army I found some very agreeable, and all were very attentive to me. Liuts. Warner & Hammund, the principal managers of affairs did themselves credit in their interested and active movements to make the time pass agreeably to their visitors.

El Senor Vicario [the priest] was there to grace the gay halls with his priestly robes—he is a man rather short of statu[r]e, but that is made up in width, which not a little care for the stomach lends an assisting hand in completing the man. There was "Dona Tula" the principal *monte-bank keeper*[2] in Sant Fé, a stately dame of a certain age, the possessor of a portion of that shrewd sense and fascinating manner necessary to allure the wayward, inexperienced youth to the hall of final ruin. . . . There, too, circling giddily through the dance, Cpt. M[oore] of [First] Dragoons; if necessary we can be sure of at least one person to testify to the "virtues or vices" of what has been graphically called "the ingredient." There in that corner sits a dark-eyed Senora with a human footstool; in other words with her servant

---

[2]*monte-bank keeper.* Monte was a card game. Dona Tula ran a gambling hall where the game was played and therefore had money at hand to lend. She loaned the U.S. army in Santa Fe one thousand dollars.

under her feet—a custom I am told, when they attend a place of the kind to take a servant along and while sitting to use them as an article of furniture.

The music consisted of a gingling guitar, and violin with the occasional effort to chime in an almost unearthly voice. *Las Senoras y Senoritas* [the ladies and girls—young ladies] were dressed in silks, satins, ginghams & lawns, embroidered crape shawls, fine rabozos— and decked with various showy ornaments, such as hugh necklaces, countless rings, combs, bows of ribbands, red and other coloured handkerchiefs, and other fine *fancy* articles. This is a short sketch of a Mexican ball. Liuts Warner & Hammond called this evening to see how I *enjoyed* the dance (not that I joined [in] it myself).

30

AMERICAN OFFICER

The Virtues of Mexican Women

September 1846

This letter was written by an anonymous officer and published in war correspondent Thomas Bangs Thorpe's 1847 book Our Army at Monterey,[1] *part of his two-volume chronicle of General Zachary Taylor's military campaigns. Note the contrasting depictions of Mexican men and women as seen through the lens of American notions of gender.*

The social life of the Montereyans exhibits a higher order of refinement than had been witnessed by our troops, who had proceeded from Matamoros. It was evident that as "the interior" was approached, the people became more hardy and intelligent. No doubt the temperate climate caused exertions to be made incompatible with the heats

[1]Although the author spells the Mexican city of Monterrey with one *r*, it is generally spelled with two *r*s.

From Thomas Bangs Thorpe, *Our Army at Monterey* (Philadelphia: Carey and Hart, 1847), 121–23.

of the lower lands. The rich mines, too, have their influence upon the inhabitants of Monterey; with the means there comes the desire for luxurious refinement.

Display is the ruling passion; a ride in the plaza, or a prominent place at church, seems to be among the highest ambitions. To an American, a Mexican gentleman appears incommoded with trappings, and absurd from his gaudy display. On horseback or on foot, there is a theatrical air that betrays the most superficial thinker and the most profound vanity. The character of the men of Mexico is familiar with our people, but the female population are of a higher order of beings, and most worthy of admiration; they are possessed of all the good qualities so wanting in the opposite sex.

The Mexican women of every class are brave and humane. They resented the surrender of Matamoros, and denounced the members of their own army to their faces. At Monterey, the women wrote letters to different departments, charging their own troops with cowardice. They have always shown every disposition to make any sacrifices in the defense of their country; and there is an almost certainty that a woman commanded a body of Lancers at Monterey, and was distinguished for her bravery. In the principal grave-yard near the city of Mexico, there is to be seen the tomb of Donna Maria Vicario de Quitana, of whom it is stated, that "she preferred to leave her convent and join the standard of her country, under which she performed many feats of valor." Over the battle-field, on the suburbs of Monterey, they hovered, as ministering angels, and were seen to extend their kind services to our own wounded, who were afterwards lanced by the Mexican troops.

In the whole of Mexico, in fact in all the Spanish American countries, the women are superior to the men, both in body and mind. Comparatively uneducated, they perform their social duties with a higher regard to virtue than the moral standard of their nation demands. The higher classes are idle from habit, yet they make the hours agreeable by entwining their hair with blossoms, or making delicate embroideries. They while away the day in the hammock and in dressing for public display. In society, they converse pertly with their tongues and scandalize with the movement of their fans. They take an active part in the political strifes with which they are surrounded, and are justly credited with originating many of the revolutions that distract their country. With all their superior traits, they have weaknesses, as have all humanity.

A Mexican woman, high or low, rich or poor, bestows all of her choicest sympathy upon her feet. To be beautiful otherwise, and yet not have small feet, is but vanity and vexation of spirit; bright eyes, virtue, and mind, are all secondary; hence it is that Mexican women have an intellectuality about their extremities truly admirable to behold. In walking, sitting, or praying in the cathedral, the satin pointed slipper occupies the eye, and seems ever to be prominent and worthy of admiration.

Of the best society of Monterey, our troops have had few opportunities of judging. Society, in fact, is broken up by the miseries entailed by war, and the want of a community of languages, together. The peculiar relation of conqueror and conquered, makes, save in extraordinary cases, a proper appreciation of Mexican society impossible. It seems, however, to be in the order of Providence, that these women, so justly to be admired, are to become wives and mothers of a better race.

31

HENRY WILLIAM HERBERT

Pierre the Partisan: A Tale of the Mexican Marches

1848

In this war novel, popular writer Henry William Herbert relays the adventures of the multitalented Pierre, who encounters a unit of American dragoons, guides them out of danger, and later entertains his new friends with many stories. In this tale, Herbert reveals his own racialized view of Mexicans.

Pierre sat erect in his saddle, gazing with his keen dark eye into the recesses of the forest, his left hand raised to his ear, for he had let fall his reins on the disciplined charger's neck, and his cocked rifle ready in the right.

From Henry William Herbert, *Pierre the Partisan: A Tale of the Mexican Marches* (New York: F. A. Brady, 1848), 22–26.

The next instant, a single Mexican came into view, wheeling his small but fiery horse round the thicket, which had sheltered their encampment, at full gallop. . . .

. . . He did not at first observe the Partisan, so motionless did he stand, backed by a thick clump of thorny bushes which gave no relief to his dark charger and sad-colored garments, but galloped fiercely forward, sparring his horse violently, and evidently following the track of the party which he was pursuing, and which he probably believed to be far more remote than it indeed was. . . .

. . . Now the ranchero—for such he seemed to be—was within forty yards of Pierre, when he saw the horse, the man, the leveled rifle—when he recognized the being he most feared on earth—the far-famed Partisan. Wheeling his horse in an instant, by dint of his cruel massive bit, which threw him on his haunches, as if by magic, the terrified wretch turned to fly. . . .

. . . Gathering up the reins in his left hand, [Pierre] gave Emperor the spur so suddenly that he bounded six feet into the air, with all his feet together, and dashed at once into his tearing gallop.

Meanwhile the rider had uncoiled the lasso, which hung from the pummel of his saddle, and whirling it around his head in the true Spanish fashion, thundered along in pursuit of the fugitive at a tremendous pace.

The Mexican had, it is true, some fifty yards the start of his pursuer, and knowing that he was riding for his life, or at least for his liberty, plied his long-roweled spurs with desperate energy.

The animal he rode was swift and active, though small and low of size, being descended probably from the old Andalusian blood, and the best in Europe from its greater admixture with the Moorish strain, which was imported to this continent by its first conquerors [the Spanish].

But fleet and high-spirited as it was, it had not the least chance of contending against the vastly superior power and longer stride of the Anglo-American thorough-bred. . . .

The noble horse, well knowing his part in what was to ensue, stopped dead short in his full career, the Partisan throwing himself back in the stirrups, and sitting as perfectly unmoved by the shock, as if he had been a portion of the charger he bestrode.

But that was not the only feat which the instinct and experience of the gallant beast had taught him; for, bracing every muscle of his wiry and elastic frame, he leaned so far over on the side opposite to that whence the lasso had been sped, that he would have fallen, but for the violent resistance which ensued instantly.

Aimed by an eagle eye, and launched by a master hand, the terrible noose encircled both the forelegs of the Mexican horse as he sprang forward; was drawn taut on the instant by the very speed of the trammeled captive, and hurled horse and rider headlong to the earth, with a violence which left both for an instant senseless.

The tremendous force of such a check can better be conceived than described: but it was so great that in spite of the superior weight and bone of the Emperor, it would probably have cast him also to the ground, but for the position in which he received the shock; and, as it was, he was dragged several yards, his hoofs literally plowing up the forest soil in deep furrows before he could recover perfect control of his limbs.

The next moment Pierre had leaped from his saddle and sprang upon his captive almost before he opened his eyes on recovering from his terrible fall.

Ere he had regained his senses, he was disarmed, and his arms pinioned so far behind him, that, although he could use his hands and forearms from the elbow, he could not raise them to his head, or make any attempt to either strike or parry.

His horse was next released from the lasso, and allowed to recover his feet, which it did, trembling with terror, and sweating at every pore, but not nearly so much shaken or bruised by so violent a fall as might have been expected, owing probably to the softness of the ground.

The noose of the lasso was now transferred to the neck of the unhappy Mexican, whose swarthy features had changed to a sort of greenish-yellow hue, standing as he did in imminent terror of instant death by strangulation, of which, indeed, he appeared to be in no small risk.

"Life!" he cried, piteously, in Spanish, "life! for the love of God, and the most holy Virgin! For charity! give me my life, Senor American!"

"Mount your horse, fool!" replied the Partisan, sternly, "who the devil do you think would trouble himself to take such a miserable life as yours. Mount your horse, I say, and cease your howling, or I will send my knife through your coward heart!" He also used the Spanish tongue, which he spoke not only idiomatically, but with all the ease and fluency of a native; and to enforce his threats, he laid his hand with a grim smile on the hilt of his formidable wood-knife.

32

OUR JONATHAN

Song of the Volunteers

1846

War songs were compiled and distributed in many pocket-size books. The first to appear was Philadelphian William M'Carty's National Songs, Ballads, and Other Patriotic Poetry Chiefly Relating to the War of 1846, *published soon after the conflict's initial battles. This song, originally attributed to an unknown person identified as "Our Jonathan," was first published in the* Philadelphia Globe *and later included in M'Carty's songbook. Sung to the tune of the minstrel melody "Old Dan Tucker," it was performed by George Washington Dixon at the May 20, 1846, pro-war rally in New York City. Note how Mexicans are depicted in the song and the outcome it suggests for the war.*

> The Mexicans are on our soil,
> In war they wish us to embroil;
> They've tried their best and worst to vex us
> By murdering our brave men in Texas.
> > *Chorus*—We're on our way to Rio Grande,
> > On our way to Rio Grande,
> > On our way to Rio Grande,
> > And with arms they'll find us handy.
>
> We are the boys who fear no noise,
> We'll leave behind us all our joys
> To punish those half-savage scamps,
> Who've slain our brethren in their camps.
> > *Chorus*—We're on our way to Matamoras,
> > On our way to Matamoras,

From William M'Carty, ed., *National Songs, Ballads, and Other Patriotic Poetry Chiefly Relating to the War of 1846* (Philadelphia: W. M'Carty, 1846), 35–38.

On our way to Matamoras,
And we'll drive them all before us. . . .

We'll cross the famous Rio Grande,
Engage the villains hand to hand,
And punish them for all their sins
By stripping off their yellow skins.
We're on our way, &c. . . .

Meanwhile our brethren in the west
Will for our nation do their best,
And when they've ended their long journey
Our flag will float in California.
We're on our way, &c.

The world is wide, our views are large,
We're sailing on in Freedom's barge,
Our God is good and we are brave,
From tyranny the world we'll save.
We're on our way, &c. . . .

We go for equal rights and laws,
We'll bravely fight in Freedom's cause,
And though the world may take the field,
To tyrants we will never yield.
We're on our way, &c.

The God of War, the mighty Mars,
Has smiled upon our stripes and stars;
And spite of any ugly rumors
We'll vanquish all the Montezumas!
We're on our way to Matamoras,
On our way to Matamoras,
On our way to Matamoras,
And we'll conquer all before us!

33

JOHN GREENLEAF WHITTIER

The Angels of Buena Vista

1847

Born in 1807 in Haverhill, Massachusetts, poet John Greenleaf Whittier was a Quaker, ardent abolitionist, and pacifist. Inspired by a newspaper account of Mexican women tending to their wounded soldiers following the Battle of Buena Vista, Whittier wrote this poignant poem, whose romantic appeal ensured its popularity.

Speak and tell us, our Ximena,[1] looking northward far away,
O'er the camp of the invaders, o'er the Mexican array,
Who is losing? who is winning? are they far or come they near?
Look abroad, and tell us, sister, whither rolls the storm we hear.

"Down the hills of Angostura[2] still the storm of battle rolls;
Blood is flowing, men are dying; God have mercy on their souls!"
Who is losing? who is winning?—"Over hill and over plain,
I see but smoke of cannon clouding through the mountain rain."

Holy Mother! keep our brothers! Look, Ximena, look once more:
"Still I see the fearful whirlwind rolling darkly as before,
Bearing on, in strange confusion, friend and foeman, foot and horse,
Like some wild and troubled torrent sweeping down its mountain
course."

Look forth once more, Ximena! "Ah! the smoke has rolled away;
And I see the Northern rifles gleaming down the ranks of gray.
Hark! that sudden blast of bugles! there the troop of Minon wheels;
There the Northern horses thunder, with the cannon at their heels.

[1]*Ximena*: The name of the woman who is tending to the injured.
[2]*Angostura*: Another name for the area where the battle of Buena Vista took place.

From John Greenleaf Whittier, *The Early Poems of John Greenleaf Whittier with Biographical Sketch by N. H. Dole* (New York: Thomas Y. Crowell, 1893), 329–33.

"Jesu, pity! how it thickens! now retreat and now advance!
Right against the blazing cannon shivers Puebla's[3] charging lance!
Down they go, the brave young riders; horse and foot together fall;
Like a plowshare in the fallow, through them plow the Northern ball."

Nearer came the storm and nearer, rolling fast and frightful on:
Speak, Ximena, speak and tell us, who has lost, and who has won?
"Alas! alas! I know not; friend and foe together fall,
O'er the dying rush the living: pray, my sisters, for them all!"

"Lo! the wind the smoke is lifting: Blessed Mother,[4] save my brain!
I can see the wounded crawling slowly out from heaps of slain.
Now they stagger, blind and bleeding; now they fall, and strive to rise;
Hasten, sisters, haste and save them, lest they die before our eyes!"

[3]*Puebla*: A city and state in the central east portion of Mexico.
[4]*Blessed Mother*: The Virgin Mary.

34

JAMES RUSSELL LOWELL

The Biglow Papers

1846

James Russell Lowell, a twenty-seven-year-old Boston poet, literary critic, and abolitionist, wrote what became known as The Biglow Papers *to protest Massachusetts governor George Briggs's call for volunteers following the declaration of war against Mexico. The poems in this collection were written in a New England dialect to depict fictional character Hosea Biglow's views on the conflict.*

Thrash away, you'll *hev* to rattle
  On them kittle drums o' yourn,—
'Taint a knowin' kind o' cattle
  Thet is ketched with mouldy corn;

James Russell Lowell, *The Biglow Papers* (London: Routledge, 1886), 48–50.

Put in stiff, you fifer feller,
    Let folks see how spry you be, —
Guess you'll toot till you are yeller
    'Fore you git ahold o' me!

Thet air flag's a leetle rotten,
    Hope it aint your Sunday's best; —
Fact! it takes a sight o' cotton
    To stuff out a soger's[1] chest:
Sence we farmers hev to pay fer 't,
    Ef you must wear humps like these,
Sposin' you should try salt hay fer 't,
    It would du ez slick ez grease.

'T would n't suit them Southun fellers,
    They're a dreffle graspin' set,
We must ollers blow the bellers
    Wen they want their irons het;
May be it's all right ez preachin',
    But *my* narves it kind o' grates,
Wen I see the overreachin'
    O' them nigger-driving' States.

Them thet rule us, them slave-traders,
    Haint they cut a thunderin' swarth,
(Helped by Yankee renegaders,)
    Thru the vartu o' the North!
We begin to think it's nater
    To take sarse an' not be riled; —
Who'd expect to see a tater
    All on eend at bein' biled?

Ez fer war, I call it murder, —
    There you hev it plain an' flat;
I don't want to go no furder
    Than my Testyment fer that;
God hez sed so plump an' fairly,
    It's ez long ez it is broad,
An' you've gut to git up airly
    Ef you want to take in God.

[1] *soger's*: Soldier's.

'Taint your eppyletts an' feathers
   Make the thing a grain more right;
'Taint afollerin' your bell-wethers
   Will excuse ye in His sight;
Ef you take a sword an' dror it,
   An' go stick a feller thru,
Guv'ment aint to answer for it,
   God'll send the bill to you.

Wut's the use o' meetin-goin'
   Every Sabbath, wet or dry,
Ef it's right to go amowin'
   Feller-men like oats an' rye?
I dunno but wut it's pooty
   Trainin' round in bobtail coats,—
But it's curus Christian dooty
   This ere cuttin' folks's throats.

They may talk o' Freedom's airy
   Tell they're pupple in the face,—
It's a grand gret cemetary
   Fer the barthrights of our race;
They jest want this Californy
   So's to lug new slave-states in
to abuse ye, an' to scorn ye,
   An' to plunder ye like sin.

Aint it cute to see a Yankee
   Take sech everlastin' pains,
All to git the Devil's thankee,
   Helpin' on 'em weld their chains?
Wy, it's jest ez clear ez figgers,
   Clear ez one an' one make two,
Chaps thet make black slaves o' niggers
   Want to make wite slaves o' you.

35

GEORGE WILKINS KENDALL

The Mexican Joan of Arc

January 12, 1847

The Spirit of the Times *was a New York–based weekly periodical that served as a clearinghouse for articles that might appeal to upper-class readers. In this article, which originally appeared in the* New Orleans Picayune, *George Wilkins Kendall, the most widely known correspondent of the U.S. war with Mexico, augmented the description of a Monterrey woman known as Dos Amades, who led a group of lancers in a battle there. Notice how gender and race came into play in the depiction of Dos Amades.*

In a recent letter from "G de L," he speaks of the recognition of a deserter from our army, as he marched out of Monterey [*sic*] with the Mexican force. . . . "G de L" also spoke of a certain Dos Amades, a female who is said to have commanded a company of Lancers at the battle of Monterey [*sic*]. He says:

> Seized with a patriotic spirit, she unsexed herself and dressed in a full suit of a captain of lancers she desired to be led against the foe; and swore that she would never yield, until the "Northern Barbarians" were driven from her natal land, or until she had shed her last drop of blood in defense of her native country. Previous to our attack, she was paraded before the troops, and greatly excited and augmented their courage. She harangued them and desired to be posted at that spot where the first shot should fall, and where the thickest of the ballet should wage. It is reported that on the 21st she led the charge of lancers which proved fatal to some of our command—among the number the lamented Field. There's an example of heroism worthy the days of old! It has remained for Mexico to produce a second Joan of Arc, but not like her, successful. I would have given a great deal to have seen her ladyship.

George Wilkins Kendall, "Irish Deserter and Mexican Joan of Arc," *Spirit of the Times*, January 2, 1847, 534.

104

After quoting the paragraph above from his paper, Mr. Kendall adds,
The adventures of this girl, who was said to be the daughter of a
former Governor of Nuevo Leon, were the common talk of Monterey
[*sic*] a few days after the battle. It was said that, fatigued and worn out
by her exertions, she knocked at the window of a house in the *Calle
de Morelos* on the night of the 23rd September, not knowing that some
of Hay's[1] Texans had poked their way into the very room. The lady of
the house, who was an intimate friend of the girl, quietly told her the
circumstance, when she remounted her horse and rode towards the
Grand Plaza. The suspension of hostilities on the following morning
induced her to doff her uniform and return to her family, and after
that we heard no farther of her movements. Should some Mexican
writer recount the exploits of this Maid of Monterey [*sic*], for there is
little doubt she was foremost in many of the fights, they might throw
in the shade the feats of the celebrated Maid of Saragossa.[2]

[1]John Coffee (Jack) Hays, who led a regiment of Texas Rangers during the Mexican War.
[2]*Maid of Saragossa*: Maria Agustín fought against the French invaders of Saragossa,
Spain, in 1808. In 1812 Lord Byron wrote of her exploits in his poem "Childe Harolde's
Pilgrimage."

36

SAMUEL E. CHAMBERLAIN

My Confession

1855

*Samuel Chamberlain was born in 1829 in Center Harbor, New Hamp-
shire. When he was a boy, his family moved to Boston, where his father
died in 1844. In that year Samuel left home and settled in Illinois. Following the Battles of Palo Alto and Resaca de la Palma in early May
1846, Chamberlain joined the Alton Guards, a volunteer regiment from
Illinois. Throughout the war Chamberlain carried a sketchbook and drew
pictures as gifts for his fellow soldiers. Later when he sat down to write*

From Samuel E. Chamberlain, *My Confession* (New York: Harper and Brothers, 1956),
124–25.

his book, he included one hundred large drawings and decorated the
written pages with colored initials, pen-and-ink vignettes, and richly
worked script. In his war memoir, Samuel Chamberlain offered vivid
depictions of the conflict's battles. Written between 1855 and 1861, the
manuscript remained in obscurity for nearly a century until a collector
discovered it in a Connecticut antiques shop in the 1940s. Excerpts
appeared in the popular magazine Life *before the entire manuscript was*
published in 1956. In 1854 Chamberlain moved back to Boston, mar-
ried, and raised a family. He eventually became a prominent citizen,
held public office, and became a brevet brigadier general at the end of
the Civil War. He died in 1908.

I really believe that the battle of Buena Vista would have been lost to
us if General [Zachary] Taylor had been allowed to have his own way,
at any time during the day of the 23rd [of February].

The Mexicans had a heavy battery of three guns, manned by Irish
deserters from our army. These desperadoes were organized as a battalion known as the Battalia San Patricio, or Legion of Saint Patrick;
the commander was the notorious Reilly, who ranked as a Colonel in
the Mexican Army. A beautiful green silk banner waved over their
heads; on it glittered a silver cross and a golden harp, embroidered by
the hands of the fair nuns of San Luis Potosi. The deserters pitched
their shells into every part of the field, some bursting in the road a
good mile in our rear.

General Taylor ordered Lieutenant Rucker to take that "d——d
battery." (The old gentleman was sometimes slightly profane.) Now
the order was very easy to give, but rather difficult to execute, but
such men as Rucker, Carleton and Buford are not apt to hesitate in the
face of danger, so we tightened our saddle girths, and stripped ourselves of all encumbrances such as greatcoats, haversacks, nosebags,
etc. With a firm grip on our Sabres, down a ravine we went at a trot,
cheered by Sherman's battery as we passed under the muzzles of
their guns, and were soon hid from the sight of both armies by the
banks of the ravine. We passed many dead and wounded Mexicans in
the gulches, and more than one poor wounded wretch was trampled
to death beneath our horses' hoofs. We moved up another ravine and
rising the bank, saw through the dense cloud of smoke and dust, the
glittering cross that waved over the deserters' guns.

Re-forming our platoons, we went for them at speed. I thought we
would capture the guns without much trouble, as the pieces were so

elevated that the shots passed high over our heads. Just as we were on them, the Bugler sounded to the "right," in the nick of time for our wheeling flank to clear a yawning chasm full ten yards wide that opened in front of the battery. We were soon under shelter in the ravine, and we kept down this to the road, and struck for the pass. The road was literally blocked by the heaps of dead horses and men moved down by the fire of Washington's battery in the cavalry charge that morning.

The battle was raging furiously all along the line as we regained our old position on the plateau when suddenly a heavy shower burst on us. The wind blew a gale and the thunder was fearful; peal after peal burst over us as if to mock our puny artillery. For a few minutes all was darkness from the thick clouds of dust driven along by the violent blast. The firing ceased on both sides, as if by mutual consent. The rain was as cold as ice, but was favorable to us as the wind was driving it with great force in the faces of our foes. The shower lasted some fifteen minutes, clearing off as suddenly as it came up, the sun came out, and a magnificent rainbow spanned the valley. We hailed this as a good omen, and our guns renewed their fire.

37

RAMÓN ALCARAZ

Description of the Battle of Buena Vista

1850

Ramón Alcaraz, a Mexican journalist who followed the Mexican army during the war, was one of fifteen authors of Apuntes para la historia de la guerra entre México y Los Estados Unidos, *published in Mexico in 1848. Compiled by Mexican officers, politicians, and journalists as a step toward writing a history of the war, the book was translated into English by Albert C. Ramsey and published in the United States in 1850. In one*

From Ramón Alcaraz et al., *The Other Side; or, Notes for the History of the War between Mexico and the United States*, trans. and ed. Albert C. Ramsey (New York: J. Wiley, 1850), 127–28.

*selection, Alcaraz described the Mexican army's experience in the bloodi-
est battle in the war's northern theater.*

After the second combat, which was in the morning between ten and
eleven, a light drizzling rain fell. Our troops now took some rest and at
twelve returned to march again upon the positions of the enemy. The
Sappers[1] and other corps who were in reserve having at this time
already turned to engage in the battle, General [Zachary] Taylor believed our left was weak. He therefore advanced some forces in that
direction, who met with an unconquerable resistance. The brigade of
[General Anastasio] Torrejon charged upon them, and they lost many
officers and soldiers. The action became general; our line advanced;
the light corps, who in the course of the battle had made the troops
which they met give way, and were now at the very extreme end of
the brow of a hill, closed with the enemy. Again the affray[2] became desperate, the dead and wounded increased on both sides; the one attacked
gallantly, the other defended bravely; none yielded; the combat was
prolonged for whole hours, and at the end only after unheard of efforts did they succeed in rolling the enemy to their last position. Two
more of their [artillery] pieces and a field forge[3] fell into our hands.

At this time there came on a heavy shower of rain, and the troops,
dead with fatigue, halted. Taylor having tenaciously receded from hill
to hill, and losing all, after an obstinate resistance, prepared to make
his final stand before yielding the palm of victory. But the battle had
ceased; the charge feebly made was the last stroke of our forces. The
enemy did not believe themselves routed, for so well had they lost all
their positions, except one, which was sufficient still to present a hostile attitude, that they feigned the glory of having conquered. On our
part the army was proclaimed victorious, alleging in proof the trophies
captured, the positions taken, and the divisions vanquished. The truth
is, our arms routed the Americans in all the encounters, and so far the
issue of the battle was favorable to us. There had been three partial
triumphs, but not a complete victory.

During the action the brigade of General [José Vicente] Miñon was
in the rear of Taylor's army, sometimes near to Buena Vista, sometimes

[1] *Sappers*: Soldiers employed in building and repairing fortifications.
[2] *affray*: Fray; fight.
[3] *field forge*: A traveling forge that carried the supplies necessary to shoe horses and
to repair and preserve carriages and harnesses.

to Saltillo. Its inaction has given rise to a warm controversy between Generals [Antonio López de] Santa Anna and Miñon, into which we will not enter, for our principal object is to refer to events as they transpired, without taking part in discussions which have arisen from them.

The nation has cause to lament the serious losses in this battle. There the blood of her bravest sons flowed copiously, and forty officers were borne off wounded. Among the killed we must mention the Lieut.-colonels D. Francisco Berra and D. Felix Azoños; commandante of battalion, D. Julian de los Rios, and commandantes of squadron, D. Ignacio Peña, D. Juan Lullando, and D. José Santoyo, who fell upon the field of battle.

38

CITIZENS OF NEW MEXICO

Report to the President of Mexico

September 26, 1846

A month after Governor Manuel Armijo fled Santa Fe and allowed the U.S. Army to invade New Mexico, the citizens of the territory wrote to the president of Mexico reporting on their circumstances.

Since the middle of last June His Excellency Sr. Armijo knew beyond doubt that the [American] expedition would arrive this year. He also received definite news of the said expedition on July 10th, through the four merchants from this Department[1] whom we have mentioned. Very early in August, Sr. Don Pío Sambrano arrived at this city and he, too, told him that the said expedition was on the road. If he had mustered the citizenry in July which he gathered later; if he had marched

---

[1]*Department*: A Mexican administrative unit similar to a U.S. territory.

From "Notes and Documents," *New Mexico Historical Review*, 26, no. 1 (January 1951): 73–75.

with it and his troops to meet the enemy then, not at the gateway of the city as he did, but at the greatest possible distance from it; if he had not allowed the more than fifty thousand pesos entering the frontier customs house of this city in July to be invested in other than the organization of the country's defense; if he had raised and trained companies for that purpose, as he had more than enough men with arms, horses, and their own equipment; if the money he collected from exempting some individuals from the campaign had been put to the same use; if he also had designated the same purpose for that collected by voluntary subscription in this city and for that which he received from the municipal funds; if he had arranged in time for the production of munitions of war, for which there was more than enough powder and lead in the Department; if he had purchased some food supplies to have in reserve; if he had taken advantage of the good disposition which all of the citizens exhibited in the junta which he convoked in this city, in which they offered him their lives and property; if he had accepted the generous offers of the same which the visiting vicar and various other wealthy residents of the Department had made him; and finally, if he had personally marched to the frontier with the forces which he could have had at his disposal: without doubt we would have fought the invaders, firing at them day and night. We would have managed to surprise them and seize their horses, to ambush them in the waterless deserts, to burn their pasturage, to take advantage of the almost inaccess[i]ble mountain passes which they had to cross, and, finally, we would have made some kind of resistance. It would be a great deal for us to venture that victory would have crowned our efforts, but at least we would have had the honor of having tried. Nothing, absolutely nothing was done. And Sr. Armijo can say full well: *I have lost everything, including honor.*

More than four thousand men are witness to the deeds which we have related. The entire Department is convinced of the truth of our assertions, and our honor, more than any other consideration, has obliged us to send Your Excellency this repetitious manifesto so that at no time may it be believed that we have been a disgrace to the Mexican nation, with which we are bound by so many ties. We offer Your Excellency our most distinguished respects and attentive considerations.

God and Liberty. Santa Fe. September 26, 1846.

39

RALPH W. KIRKHAM

Description of the City of Puebla

June 28, 1847

Born in Springfield, Massachusetts, in 1821, Ralph W. Kirkham attended West Point and was commissioned as a second lieutenant in the U.S. infantry. He began his journal in March 1847 en route to Veracruz. A month later, he joined General Winfield Scott's forces there. Kirkham described his impressions of Mexico and its people and was especially good at describing interactions between the American military and Mexican citizens.

June 28, 1847. Puebla.

I witnessed today the funeral of a little girl about eight years of age. I saw the procession coming down the street as I was standing on the balcony in the second story of my quarters. The procession was led by some ten or twelve boys who carried long, lighted wax candles. . . .

I have every day remarked the great fondness of the Mexicans for flowers. You can scarcely find a house without some few, and many, even of the poorer classes, have a great variety. Most of the houses have balconies or projections from the windows in which they usually keep their flower pots and vases, and as the temperature in this latitude is equable, they require little care besides watering in the dry season.

The Mexicans are also passionately fond of birds, not only singing birds, but a variety of others. Mocking and canary birds are very common; the former can be bought when young for a mere trifle, sometimes as low as 12 1/2 cents [one *real*]. And I have seen old songsters, which would have sold for ten and twenty dollars in the United States, here offered for one or two dollars. The Mexicans seem to value them as pets. I have gone into a house of the low order of people and

From Robert Ryal Miller, ed., *The Mexican War Journal and Letters of Ralph W. Kirkham* (College Station: Texas A&M University Press, 1991), 32–34.

counted as many as ten cages, each with one and some with two birds, and perhaps some half a dozen others were perched in different parts of the room. I have also frequently noticed cats, which seemed to be on familiar terms with them, but never offered them any violence.

One other passion the Mexicans have and gratify is that for paintings and pictures. I will venture to say there is not a house or a room occupied by Mexicans in the city of Puebla which has not from one to twenty paintings and engravings. Of course many and the greater portion of them are daubs, yet there are many fine oil paintings, and all, without any exception, are on religious subjects. Most of them are heads or half lengths, and are either our Saviour or more probably the Virgin and Child.

40

GIDEON JOHNSON PILLOW

Letter to Mary Hamilton Pillow

September 28, 1847

Gideon Johnson Pillow, President James K. Polk's former law partner, was one of the influential civilians who received appointments to the rank of general when the war began. Pillow had few or no qualifications for the job, which was revealed when he recklessly led his troops at Cerro Gordo and sustained heavy losses. In the letter to his wife, Mary, excerpted here, Pillow discusses the storming of Chapultepec and relays his feelings about the war. Although he had a reputation for being vain and ambitious, this letter shows him in a different light.

My Dear Mary:
. . . In storming Chapultepec (as I stated in my last [letter], but for fear that it may not have been received, I state here) I was cut down at the very foot of the heights by a [half-pound grape] shot, which struck

Gideon Johnson Pillow to Mary Hamilton Pillow, San Marino, Calif., September 28, 1847, Huntington Library Manuscript Collection, HM 64148.

me on the left leg, just above the ankle joints—crushing the ——
base and ankle joints. I made my men pick me up and carry me forward under the fire, I reached the main citadel just as the glorious
work was consummated and saw the stars and stripes raised. . . . I
suffered greatly with my leg for 4 days and thought I would lose the
leg, but I am now happy to inform you that my leg is recuperating well
and is entirely out of danger. It will probably be slightly out of shape at
the ankle, but I do not think that the joints will be stiff or that I will
be lame. Oh my Dear Mary, it was a glorious and most brilliant
achievement. I was selected by General Scott to do the work. He told
me at the time that the fate of the army depended upon my success.
I told him that I would take Chapultepec or would be left dead
upon the field. . . . For the horror and destruction I have caused in the
last most desperate assault by which the most powerful fortification of
Mexico fell and with it the city itself, I could well have afforded to
leave both my legs except on my dear wife's accounts. But God in his
mercy has spared my life—has covered me with distinction—left me
with legs. Praise him my Dear in your songs—in your prayers—in
your heart. My own heart is full of joy and gratitude. . . .

[Mexico City] is a great city. Nothing like it in the United States.
But as yet I have not been able to see most of it. Our army has fought
almost all around and every hill [and] valley around has been stained
with the blood of our brave men. I have witnessed so much blood
shed—so much suffering. [I] have seen so many mangled [and] dead
men, that my very nature is almost changed.

Your husband is a very changed man since you knew him. For
nearly 18 months he has mingled in the fierce conflict of battle—in
the deadly strife of man's terrible rage upon the battle field—has himself actively participated in 8 battles—while he has been thus familiar
with dangers and death, [and] they have all been his companions,—
his heart is at once melted and his hardened nature at once dissolved
into love and tenderness upon the recollection of his dear wife [and]
children.

At every moment of refuge [and] relaxation from the stern duties
of his profession, the lovely images of my wife and her sweet children,
[come] . . . to his mind, . . . all his efforts . . . all the [thoughts] of the
man [and] soldier, to avoid his weakness bursting forth in floods of
tears. Oh my dear wife and children. How tenderly I love them! How
fond is my heart and yet how miserable the distance—the . . . duty
which separates me from them! . . . with great pain [and] suffering
[and] so badly that I can scarcely know it myself. To my dear Brothers

and their wives—to your father and brothers [and] my friends I desire to be affectionately remembered. A kiss to my dear wife and children. Farewell my ever affectionate Mary.

41

AMERICAN STAR

Comment on Interactions between Mexicans and Americans
November 6, 1847

The American Star *was a bilingual newspaper published by the American military in Mexico City from September 1847 to March 1848. It included official dispatches, news reports, and classified ads. This article comments on the ways in which Americans and Mexicans interacted on Mexican soil and conveys a distinct bias.*

We have taken repeated occasions to express our gratification at the evidences, which every day presents, that the Mexican people are fast learning to entertain a more just appreciation of the American character. They evince a disposition to do justice to those who have been calumniated,[1] and to extend to them the courtesies of life. We are speaking, rather, of the intelligent and cultivated portion of the citizens, than of those who give no tone to society and exert no influence upon it. Intercourse between the former and educated Americans is fast increasing. Whether at the theatre, or in the streets, it is getting to be no uncommon thing to see an American gentleman by the side of a Mexican or Spanish lady, showing her that attention and courtesy, which are the characteristics of the intercourse between ladies and gentlemen in every part of the United States. We say we rejoice in

---

[1] *calumniated*: Injured by maliciously false statements.

"Intercourse between Mexicans and Americans," *American Star*, November 6, 1847, 2.

these evidences of kindly and friendly feelings on the part of the intelligent people of the city.

And why should not accomplished Americans in this city mix in its society and make the acquaintance of Mexican and Spanish families. There are as refined and accomplished gentlemen among the officers of the American army as are to be found in the world, and there is no lady in this capital, be she Castilian, Mexican or other origin, who may not be proud of their acquaintance and friendship. They are not only gentlemen, who have been accustomed to mix in the best society at home, but they are generally accomplished, and some of them have been distinguished as statesmen, legislators, and men of letters. Brave as the Americans are on the field of battle, they are equally generous, warm-hearted and magnanimous when the battle is over. They never allow any unkind feelings, engendered by national differences, to mar the pleasures of social intercourse, and embitter the amenities of social life. It is not in their nature to permit this. They are peculiarly a social people, and take pleasure in the society of each other. No where in the world is the standard of female character higher than in the United States, and the fact is mainly attributable to the kindly intercourse between the sexes. No where in the world, also, are there more accomplished or refined ladies than in the American Republic, where the young of both sexes mingle freely in society, and exchange thoughts upon the passing events of the day. No where, it may be added, are the heroic self-devotion, loveliness, and sacrificing spirit of the female character more conspicuous. Need any educated Mexican or Spanish lady be told of this?

There is no Mexican officer, who has had any intercourse with intelligent Americans, who has not borne warm testimony to the disinterestedness and noble heartedness which are such prominent traits of the American character. The wives and sisters and mothers of such must have heard of these traits from lips that would not lie, and they must, therefore, know that the society of gallant American officers would be not a pleasure, merely, but an honor even. No mother in Mexico need covet any higher distinction for her daughter than an alliance with an accomplished American gentleman.

It has been said by a keen observer of human nature that politeness is merely benevolence in small things. It is so, and we cannot doubt that the intercourse between American gentlemen and the cultivated families of the city, will tend to develop the kindlier feelings of the heart, and soften much of the asperity of war.... Moral worth and intellectual superiority are the passports to the most refined society in

the United States. They entitle Americans to occupy the same position
in the society of this beautiful city, and, if we have formed a correct
estimate of the Mexican and Spanish character, the time is rapidly
approaching when all the courtesies of social life will be freely extended to them. Unpleasant feelings—if they have existed—are fast
passing away, and American gentlemen are beginning to be treated
with that politeness, respect and attention, by the higher circles of the
metropolis, to which their known character, reputation and accom-
plishments entitle them.

42

RAMÓN ALCARAZ

Observations on the American
Occupation of Mexico City
1850

This excerpt from The Other Side; or, Notes for the History of the War
between Mexico and the United States *presents the Mexican perspective
of the U.S. occupation of Mexico City. Contrast this depiction with the
way the occupation was presented in the* American Star *(Document 41).*

Residence of the Americans in Mexico

. . .

The American officers, proud of the conquest which they had made,
well pleased to find themselves almost in complete security in the capital of the Republic, and persuaded that an insurrection was hardly to
be apprehended, began to arrange a complete system of amusements.

From Ramón Alcaraz et al., *The Other Side; or, Notes for the History of the War between
Mexico and the United States*, trans. and ed. Albert C. Ramsey (New York: J. Wiley,
1850), 415–17.

Several actors, urged by necessity or some other motive, engaged themselves to represent some comedies. The manager of the National Theatre found no great difficulty in renting the place, and the vanquished city began to display its attractions to the conqueror. Cañete[1] was the fascination and idol of the American chiefs, and the street of the Vergara every night presented an appearance of life and animation, to which it had been accustomed, ever since the perseverance of Sr. Arbeu[2] had erected that magnificent edifice. A few teamsters and soldiers represented comedies in German and English, in the Theatre of New Mexico.

Those who were not particularly fond of theatricals, organized dancing in imitation of the fashion in the United States. A ballroom was opened in the street of the Colisco, opposite the principal theatre, another in the alley of the Balemitas, and a third, the most crowded of all, was found in the hotel of the Bella Union. The rooms of that mansion were full of officers. In the lower apartments there was gambling, on the second floor drinking saloons, billiards and halls for dancing, and those above were chiefly devoted to purposes which propriety will not permit us to mention. From nine o'clock in the evening until two or three in the morning, their orgies continued, which never had been seen before in Mexico. The Mexican fair sex were more abundant than could have been wished, consisting chiefly of wicked, and sometimes allured girls, or obliged by want to exchange their honor for a piece of bread for their families.

The officers, beyond these public measures for their own diversion, so to speak, began to scatter themselves as lodgers in all parts of Mexico, and praising the beauty of the country and the Mexican ladies, went on by degree forming acquaintances and inspiring confidence in families.

According to data which we have seen, General Scott occupied the city with only 7,000 or 8,000 men. But afterwards some new regiments of infantry and cavalry, principally volunteers, arrived from the United States, and from the garrisons on the road.

A day seldom passed in the capital, without the attention of the inhabitants being attracted to the arrival of new forces, so that in two months after the enemy's entrance into Mexico, the aspect of the city was wholly changed. From five in the morning until seven in the evening, innumerable wagons passed through the streets in all directions.

---

[1] *Cañete*: River in Mexico City.
[2] *Arbeu*: Don Francisco Arbeu, founder of the National Theatre.

Most of the convents of monks and friars were converted into quarters and hospitals, and groups of volunteers, with six-barrelled pistols and large hunting knives in their belts, traversed the city, and filled the drinking shops and cafés. The regular troops were dressed in blue, but the volunteers and the multitude of adventurers who came with the army went about with their boots over their pantaloons, and with ridiculous hats and garments, so that they looked like clowns at a carnival.

... Among the regular officers, particularly the artillery and engineers, some young men of education and study might be recognised; but the officers of volunteers in general had the same rough manners as the soldiers, whom they treated with a familiarity far from conducive to good discipline. Every observing man wondered how those bands of vicious volunteers, without discipline, without subordination, and without experience in the management of arms, or knowledge of tactics, could have conquered our battalions, who were so well trained, instructed, obedient, patient, and, to say still more, so valiant.

43

JOHN C. CALHOUN

Speech on the War with Mexico

January 4, 1848

John C. Calhoun was a member of the Democratic Party, former vice president, and U.S. Senator from South Carolina when he delivered this speech on January 4, 1848, during the "All Mexico Movement" debate. In it, he expressed his concern about the acquisition of more Mexican territory. Note Calhoun's reasons for opposing the Republic's territorial expansion.

From Clyde Wilson and Shirley Bright Cook, eds., *Papers of John C. Calhoun* (Columbia: University of South Carolina Press, 1999), 25:64–65, 68–69.

The next reason which my resolutions assign, is, that it is without example or precedent, either to hold Mexico as a province, or to incorporate her into our Union. No example of such a line of policy can be found. We have conquered many of the neighboring tribes of Indians, but we never thought of holding them in subjection—never of incorporating them into our Union. They have either been left as an independent people amongst us, or been driven into the forests.

I know further, sir, that we have never dreamt of incorporating into our Union any but the Caucasian race—the free white race. To incorporate Mexico, would be the very first instance of the kind of incorporating an Indian race; for more than half of the Mexicans are Indians, and the other is composed chiefly of mixed tribes. I protest against such a union as that! Ours, sir, is the Government of a white race. The greatest misfortunes of Spanish America are to be traced to the fatal error of placing these colored races on an equality with the white race. That error destroyed the social arrangement which formed the basis of society. The Portuguese [in Brazil] and ourselves have escaped—the Portuguese at least to some extent—and we are the only people on this continent which have made revolutions without being followed by anarchy. And yet it is professed and talked about to erect these Mexicans into a Territorial Government, and place them on an equality with the people of the United States. I protest utterly against such a project.

Sir, it is a remarkable fact, that in the whole history of man, as far as my knowledge extends, there is no instance whatever of any civilized colored races being found equal to the establishment of free popular government, although by far the largest portion of the human family is composed of these races. And even in the savage state we scarcely find them any where with such government, except it be our noble savages—for noble I will call them. They, for the most part, had free institutions, but they are easily sustained amongst a savage people. Are we to overlook this fact? Are we to associate with ourselves as equals, companions, and fellow-citizens, the Indians and mixed race of Mexico? Sir, I should consider such a thing as fatal to our institutions.

The next two reasons which I assigned, were that it would be in conflict with the genius and character of our institutions, and subversive of our free government. I take these two together, as they are so intimately connected; and now of the first—to hold Mexico in subjection. . . .

But, Mr. President, suppose all these difficulties removed; suppose these people attached to our Union, and desirous of incorporating with us, ought we to bring them in? Are they fit to be connected with us? Are they fit for self-government and for governing you? Are you, any of you, willing that your States should be governed by these twenty-odd Mexican states, with a population of about only one million of your blood, and two or three millions of mixed blood, better informed [*sic*], all the rest pure Indians, [or] a mixed blood equally ignorant and unfit for liberty, impure races, not as good as the Cherokees or Choctaws?

We make a great mistake, sir, when we suppose that all people are capable of self-government. We are anxious to force free government on all; and I see that it has been urged in a very respectable quarter, that it is the mission of this country to spread civil and religious liberty over all the world, and especially over this continent. It is a great mistake. None but people advanced to a very high state of moral and intellectual improvement are capable, in a civilized state, of maintaining free government; and amongst those who are so purified, very few, indeed, have had the good fortune of forming a constitution capable of endurance. It is a remarkable fact in the history of man, that scarcely ever have free popular institutions been formed by wisdom alone that have endured.

44

UNITED STATES AND MEXICO

Treaty of Guadalupe Hidalgo
February 1848

After much negotiation, the Treaty of Guadalupe Hidalgo was signed on February 2, 1848, by representatives of the United States and Mexico at Guadalupe Hidalgo, on the outskirts of Mexico City. Included here is the highly contested Article X, which was omitted by the U.S. Congress against Mexico's wishes.

From Charles I. Bevans, ed., *Treaties and Other International Agreements of the United States of America, 1776–1949* (Washington, D.C.: Department of State, 1972), 9:791–92, 796–97.

In the name of Almighty God:

The United States of America, and the United Mexican States, animated by a sincere desire to put an end to the calamities of the war which unhappily exists between the two Republics, and to establish upon a solid basis relations of peace and friendship, which shall confer reciprocal benefits upon the citizens of both, and assure the concord, harmony and mutual confidence, wherein the two Peoples should live, as good Neighbours, . . . have, under the protection of Almighty God, the author of Peace, arranged, agreed upon, and signed the following[.]

Treaty of Peace, Friendship, Limits and Settlement between the United States of America and the Mexican Republic

ARTICLE I. There shall be firm and universal peace between the United States of America and the Mexican Republic, and between their respective Countries, territories, cities, towns and people, without exception of places or persons.

. . .

ARTICLE VIII. Mexicans now established in territories previously belonging to Mexico, and which remain for the future within the limits of the United States, as defined by the present Treaty, shall be free to continue where they now reside, or to remove at any time to the Mexican Republic, retaining the property which they possess in the said territories, or disposing thereof and removing the proceeds wherever they please; without their being subjected, on this account, to any contribution, tax or charge whatever.

Those who shall prefer to remain in the said territories, may either retain the title and rights of Mexican citizens, or acquire those of citizens of the United States. But, they shall be under the obligation to make their election within one year from the date of the exchange of ratifications of this treaty: and those who shall remain in the said territories, after the expiration of that year, without having declared their intention to retain the character of Mexicans, shall be considered to have elected to become citizens of the United States.

In the said territories, property of every kind, now belonging to Mexicans not established there, shall be inviolably respected. The present owners, the heirs of these, and all Mexicans who may hereafter acquire said property by contract, shall enjoy with respect to it, guaranties equally ample as if the same belonged to citizens of the United States.

. . .

[The articles below were omitted from the original document and later appeared as a footnote in the printed version of the treaty.]

The United States amendment of art. IX substituted a new text. The text of art. IX as signed reads as follows:

"The Mexicans who, in the territories aforesaid, shall not preserve the character of citizens of the Mexican Republic, conformably with what is stipulated in the preceding Article, shall be incorporated into the Union of the United States, and admitted as soon as possible, according to the principles of the Federal Constitution, to the enjoyment of all the rights of citizens of the United States. In the mean time, they shall be maintained and protected in the enjoyment of their liberty, their property, and the civil rights now vested in them according to the Mexican laws. With respect to political rights, their condition shall be on an equality with that of the inhabitants of the other territories of the United States; and at least equally good as that of the inhabitants of Louisiana and the Floridas, when these provinces, by transfer from the French Republic and the Crown of Spain, became territories of the United States.

"The same most ample guaranty shall be enjoyed by all ecclesiastics and religious corporations or communities, as well in the discharge of the offices of their ministry, as in the enjoyment of their property of every kind, whether individual or corporate. This guaranty shall embrace all temples, houses and edifices dedicated to the Roman Catholic worship; as well as all property destined to it's support, or to that of schools, hospitals and other foundations for charitable or beneficent purposes. No property of this nature shall be considered as having become the property of the American Government, or as subject to be, by it, disposed of or diverted to other uses.

"Finally, the relations and communication between the Catholics living in the territories aforesaid, and their respective ecclesiastical authorities, shall be open, free and exempt from all hindrance whatever, even although such authorities should reside within the limits of the Mexican Republic, as defined by this treaty; and this freedom shall continue, so long as a new demarcation of ecclesiastical districts shall not have been made, conformably with the laws of the Roman Catholic Church."

ARTICLE X. All grants of land made by the Mexican Government or by the competent authorities, in territories previously appertaining to Mexico, and remaining for the future within the limits of the United States, shall be respected as valid, to the same extent that the same grants would be valid, if the said territories had remained within the limits of Mexico. But the grantees of lands in Texas, put in possession thereof, who, by reason of the circumstances of the country since the beginning of the troubles between Texas and the Mexican Government, may have been prevented from fulfilling all the conditions of their grants, shall be under the obligation to fulfill the said conditions within the periods limited in the same respectively; such periods to be now counted from the date of the exchange of ratifications of this treaty: in default of which the said grants shall not be obligatory upon the State of Texas, in virtue of the stipulations contained in this Article.

45

PRESIDENT MANUEL DE LA PEÑA Y PEÑA

*An Address in Support
of the Treaty of Guadalupe Hidalgo*
May 7, 1848

Manuel de la Peña y Peña, former chief justice of the Mexican Supreme Court, became acting president following Antonio López de Santa Anna's resignation on September 16, 1847. In this address, he outlined his reasons for supporting ratification of the Treaty of Guadalupe Hidalgo.

The treaty, gentlemen, now concluded by our plenipotentiaries in the city of Guadalupe is submitted to the judgment of our national representatives, of public opinion, and also to the assessment that foreign

From Cecil Robinson, ed., *The View from Chapultepec: Mexican Writers on the Mexican-American War* (Tucson: University of Arizona Press, 1989), 108–9, 111–12.

countries will make of it. The end of a war such as the one we have suffered through, with its consequent changes, is of interest to the entire world, merits the scrutiny of philosophers and statesmen, and by its very nature brings about a new period of vital importance for the Republic. The treaties which nations arrive at must, in their various aspects, come to terms with such concepts as justice, humanity, propriety, and honor, but ultimately they will be judged in terms of whether they can be characterized as beneficial or prejudicial. Consequently, opinions will vary considerably, and it is very difficult to weight the wide range of hardships among which one might choose upon the scales of cold reason and dispassionate calculation. Nevertheless, the Treaty of Guadalupe, however it might be characterized by the present generation or by those that succeed it, will not be blamed for bringing upon the liberty and sovereignty of the nation any taint of the dishonorable or the offensive, nor will it be unworthy of a noble misfortune or of any generous sentiments. The Mexican Republic has dealt with the United States and they with it as independent peoples, and the text and spirit of the negotiations, you may well believe, do not merit the charges that have been made against us during the war.

The truth is that a fertile and beautiful part of our territory is being ceded, a considerable expanse out of which flourishing states could be formed. I have no wish to obscure the truth in such solemn moments as these and much less to deny the pain which I feel at the separation from the national union of the Mexicans of Upper California and New Mexico, and I wish to consign to you in trust a testimony of the concern with which my administration has viewed these people. Be assured, gentlemen, that their future well-being has been the most serious consideration that has faced these negotiations, and if it had been possible, even more territory would have been ceded in exchange for the liberty of the Mexican populations therein. The reflection that should the war have continued their state would only have worsened has brought me the consolation of knowing that the evils they might have suffered will never be the responsibility of my administration. A war always brings with it the most deplorable changes, and a war as unfortunate as ours could not have been exempt from those sacrifices which befall, in such situations, all societies.

. . . In this foreign war, we have just seen, although in few engagements, what have been the valor and constancy of our soldiers when they have been led by honorable and confident officers. And we all have noted that the war would have had a different outcome had there been effective organization in the army and the national guard. I have not believed, nor do I believe, that the Republic is absolutely incapable of carrying on the war or of giving examples that could transmit to posterity a sense of glory. But with the same frankness and good faith I am convinced that the situation in which we find ourselves, with all circumstances considered, loudly calls for peace. The deliberation over the war is not, as some politicians believe, a matter that can be given over to experiments or adventurous sallies. The desire for military glory cannot justify the continuation of present calamities; and especially when it is considered that lacking a national navy and with the ceded territories so distant we cannot prudently expect that a continued war effort would result in favorable negotiations that would salvage our territorial integrity. On the contrary, I believe that our loss would be greater, and the conduct of the government and the congress would not be forgiven for not having prevented yet other and more horrible disasters. In our judgment, nothing should be considered that is not in conformance with the truth, and only reckless passion can characterize this sober realism as being timid or excessively cautious. The resources for a continued resistance cannot be instantly created, nor can it be conceded to the most vigorous administration that it can make the distances of such a vast extension of territory disappear or that it can agglomerate to the coastal and frontier areas all the population of the central region.

The arguments that are now made against the peace are of the same sort that were made in 1845, first against recognizing the independence of Texas and then against negotiating with the United States, as the administration of that time wished to do. Now we lament that there had not prevailed at that time a procedure for preserving the peace. The present disillusion of those men who opposed it at that time can now be of no help to the Republic in its misfortune. Being too late, such an awakening is sterile. But it can give us a lesson that we should never forget. Let us not forget it, gentlemen, and let us make a mighty effort so that our children will not damn our memory.

Contemplate what would be the confusion and anarchy into which we would see our country sink if, with the continuing of this foreign war, all the germs of discord and the fires of passion were to be aroused, as undoubtedly they would be. Already we have seen too much of social disorganization, insecurity among our people, danger along the highways, paralyzation of all the branches of public welfare, and general misery.

46

MANUEL CRESCENCIO REJÓN

Observations on the Treaty of Guadalupe Hidalgo
April 17, 1848

A liberal from Yucatán, Manuel Crescencio Rejón helped write the Mexican Constitution in 1824 and served under Presidents Herrera and Santa Anna as minister of interior and foreign affairs. Published as a broadside in 1848, "Observations on the Treaty of Guadalupe Hidalgo" expressed Rejón's strong opposition to ratification of the accord.

President Polk in his message of last December caviled[1] about the nonacquisition of territory, because he said that if we did not accept the indemnity, we could not give satisfaction in any other way, and that this amounted to a proclamation that his republic had declared war on us unjustly. But can we not with a more powerful reason object to the injustice on his side? To agree to an indemnity on his terms would make us appear to be settling for an accounting more severe and censorious than he asks from his own nation, because we would not only be renouncing the expenses we have had and the damages we have suffered, thus implicitly accepting the figments he puts forth for a case, but we would also be paying reparations for all the damages that his country has sustained, which is infinitely worse than the former. I declare that this would degrade the national character. And to accede to the second aspect which this opprobrious treaty demands—would this not amount to covering with slime a nation such as ours, which, in the face of all kinds of provocation, has refused to be provoked into combat and finally offered resistance only in order to defend its territory, something which was not understood by the province [Texas] which was the source of this disastrous war? And so we are not only supposed to remain silent while our unjust neighbors make off with

---

[1] *caviled*: Made a frivolous objection.

From Cecil Robinson, ed., *The View from Chapultepec: Mexican Writers on the Mexican-American War* (Tucson: University of Arizona Press, 1989), 95–97.

the lands which they had at first selected for themselves, but we must also pay them for coming and taking them and others as well, and finally we are expected to confess that they had a right to all of this. Oh, no! A nation which understands the extent of the sacrifice that is being demanded of it in this way prefers to perish in face of the demand. It will adopt the extremes of heroic resolve before it will consent to such disgrace and such opprobrium.

Ratification of the Treaty Would Be the Political Death of the Republic

Nevertheless, insensible to everything, our national government has entered into those negotiations which are so humiliating to us, thus committing us to grave imputations of perfidy if we should reject the treaty, which we should surely do. This government has demonstrated its misunderstanding of the nature of the institutions by which we live and has thereby brought things to the embarrassing impasse which now confronts us. The result is that we are unable to disapprove a shameful treaty without rendering our country almost defenseless against the disasters of a war which has been so disadvantageous to us because the government has not prepared the country to resist and to continue the war to a successful end. Ultimately, the very nationhood of the republic will be undermined. Now is our last chance to sustain it. Otherwise, it will disappear within ten or fifteen years with the loss of the rest of the national territory, without there being either the means or the sense of national glory with which to resist.

The truth is that in order to blunt the force of this last consideration, to calm the just fears of those who see in these negotiations the funeral of our political existence and a melancholy future for our people in the territory which they have inherited from their fathers, we must teach the necessity of bracing up our courage. The social advantages which would accrue to us by accepting a peace now have been exaggerated, as well as the ease with which we would be able to maintain our remaining territories. It would be necessary, in order to sustain such illusions, to underestimate the spirit of enterprise of the North American people in industrial and commercial pursuits, to misunderstand their history and their tendencies, and also to presuppose in our own spirit less resistance than we have already shown toward the sincere friends of progress. Only through such illusions might one maintain that the treaty would bring a change that would be advantageous to us—as has been claimed.

With the borders of our conquerors brought closer to the heart of our nation, with the whole line of the frontier occupied by them from sea to sea, with their highly developed merchant marine, and with them so versed in the system of colonization by which they attract great numbers of the laboring classes from the old world, what can we, who are so backward in everything, do to arrest them in their rapid conquests, their latest invasions? Thousands of men will come daily to establish themselves under American auspices in the new territories with which we will have obliged them. There they will develop their commerce and stockpile large quantities of merchandise brought from the upper states. They will inundate us with all this, and our own modicum of wealth, already so miserable and depleted, will in the future sink to insignificance and nothingness. We will not accomplish anything by lowering our maritime duties, abolishing our internal customshouses, or suppressing our restrictive laws. The Anglo Americans, now situated so close to our populated provinces, will provide these areas with the marvels of the world, passing them from the frontier zones to our southern states, and having withal the advantage over us of attracting our own merchants as well as our consumers, who will favor these foreigners because of the low prices at which they will be able to buy American goods.

47

NATHAN CLIFFORD

The Protocol of Querétaro

1848

Following the deletion of Article X from the Treaty of Guadalupe Hidalgo, the Mexican government requested clarification of the U.S. Senate's reasons for modifying the accord. Nathan Clifford, the newly appointed American minister to Mexico, wrote the Protocol of Querétaro to explain the alterations.

From David Hunter Miller, ed., *Treaties and Other International Acts of the United States of America* (Washington, D.C.: Government Printing Office, 1937), 5:380–81.

In the city of Querétaro on the twenty-sixth of the month of May eighteen hundred and forty-eight at a conference between Their Excellencies Nathan Clifford and Ambrose H. Sevier Commissioners of the United States of America, with full powers from their Government to make to the Mexican Republic suitable explanations in regard to the amendments which the Senate and Government of the said United States have made in the treaty of peace, friendship, limits and definitive settlement between the two Republics, signed in Guadalupe Hidalgo, on the second day of February of the present year, and His Excellency Don Luis de la Rosa, Minister of Foreign Affairs of the Republic of Mexico, it was agreed, after adequate conversation respecting the changes alluded to, to record in the present protocol the following explanations which Their aforesaid Excellencies the Commissioners gave in the name of their Government and in fulfillment of the Commission conferred upon them near the Mexican Republic.

FIRST

The [A]merican Government by suppressing the IXth article of the Treaty of Guadalupe and substituting the III[d] article of the Treaty of Louisiana did not intend to diminish in any way what was agreed upon by the aforesaid article IXth in favor of the inhabitants of the territories ceded by Mexico. Its understanding that all of that agreement is contained in the IIId article of the Treaty of Louisiana. In consequence, all the privileges and guarantees, civil, political and religious, which would have been possessed by the inhabitants of the ceded territories, if the IXth article of the Treaty had been retained, will be enjoyed by them without any difference under the article which has been substituted.

SECOND

The American Government by suppressing the Xth article of the Treaty of Guadalupe did not in any way intend to annul the grants of lands made by Mexico in the ceded territories. These grants, notwithstanding the suppression of the article of the Treaty, preserve the legal value which they may possess; and the grantees may cause their legitimate titles to be acknowledged before the [A]merican tribunals.

Conformably to the law of the United States, legitimate titles to every description of property personal and real, existing in the ceded territories, are those which were legitimate titles under the Mexican law in California and New Mexico up to the 13th of May 1846, and in Texas up to the 2d March 1836.

THIRD

The Government of the United States by suppressing the concluding paragraph of article XIIth of the Treaty, did not intend to deprive the Mexican Republic of the free and unrestrained faculty of ceding, conveying or transferring at any time (as it may judge best) the sum of the twel[v]e millions of dollars which the same Government of the United States is to deliver in the places designated by the amended article.

And these explanations having been accepted by the Minister of the Foreign Affairs of the Mexican Republic, he declared in name of his Government that with the understanding conveyed by them, the same Government would proceed to ratify the Treaty of Guadalupe as modified by the Senate and Government of the United States. In testimony of which their Excellencies the aforesaid Commissioners and the Minister have signed and sealed in quintuplicate the present protocol.

48

U.S. CONGRESS

California Land Act

March 3, 1851

Senator William Gwin pressed Congress to pass the California Land Act in 1851 both to satisfy American squatters in California and because he believed that the majority of Mexican land titles were flawed. This legislation hastened the disenfranchisement of Californios and ensured the establishment of Anglo hegemony in California.

From George Minot, ed., *U.S. Statutes at Large* (Boston: Charles C. Little and James Brown, 1851), 9:631–33.

Act to Ascertain and Settle the Private Land Claims in the State of California

Be it enacted by the Senate and House of Representatives of the United States of America in Congress assembled, That for the purpose of ascertaining and settling private land claims in the State of California, a commission shall be, and is hereby, constituted, which shall consist of three commissioners, to be appointed by the President of the United States, by and with the advice and consent of the Senate, which commission shall continue for three years from the date of this act, unless sooner discontinued by the President of the United States.

. . .

SEC. 8.   *And be it further enacted,* That each and every person claiming lands in California by virtue of any right or title derived from the Spanish or Mexican government, shall present the same to the said commissioners when sitting as a board, together with such documentary evidence and testimony of witnesses as the said claimant relies upon in support of such claims; and it shall be the duty of the commissioners, when the case is ready for hearing, to proceed promptly to examine the same upon such evidence, and upon the evidence produced in behalf of the United States, and to decide upon the validity of the said claim, and, within thirty days after such decision is rendered, to certify the same, with the reasons on which it is founded, to the district attorney of the United States in and for the district in which such decision shall be rendered.

SEC. 9.   *And be it further enacted,* That in all cases of the rejection or confirmation of any claim by the board of commissioners, it shall and may be lawful for the claimant or the district attorney, in behalf of the United States, to present a petition to the District Court of the district in which the land claimed is situated, praying the said court to review the decision of the said commissioners, and to decide on the validity of such claim; and such petition, if presented by the claimant, shall set forth fully the nature of the claim and the names of the original and present claimants, and shall contain a deraignment[1] of the claimant's title, together with a transcript of the report of the board of commissioners, and of the documentary evidence and testimony of the

---

[1] *deraignment:* Justification or proof.

witnesses on which it was founded; and such petition, if presented by the district attorney in behalf of the United States, shall be accompanied by a transcript of the report of the board of commissioners, and of the papers and evidence on which it was founded, and shall fully and distinctly set forth the grounds on which the said claim is alleged to be invalid, a copy of which petition, if the same shall be presented by a claimant, shall be served on the district attorney of the United States, and, if presented in behalf of the United States, shall be served on the claimant or his attorney; and the party upon whom such service shall be made shall be bound to answer the same within a time to be prescribed by the judge of the District Court; and the answer of the claimant to such petition shall set forth fully the nature of the claim, and the names of the original and present claimants, and shall contain a deraignment of the claimant's title; and the answer of the district attorney in behalf of the United States shall fully and distinctly set forth the grounds on which the said claim is alleged to be invalid, copies of which answers shall be served upon the adverse party thirty days before the meeting of the court, and thereupon, at the first term of the court thereafter, the said case shall stand for trial, unless, on cause shown, the same shall be continued by the court.

SEC. 10.   *And be it further enacted*, That the District Court shall proceed to render judgment upon the pleadings and evidence in the case, and upon such further evidence as may be taken by order of the said court, and shall, on application of the party against whom judgment is rendered, grant an appeal to the Supreme Court of the United States, on such security for costs in the District and Supreme Court, in case the judgment of the District Court shall be affirmed, as the said court shall prescribe; and if the court shall be satisfied that the party desiring to appeal is unable to give such security, the appeal may be allowed without security.

49

CALIFORNIA LANDOWNERS

*Petition to the Honorable Senate
and House of Representatives
of the United States of America*

February 11, 1859

In this petition, fifty-three Californio landowners informed the U.S. Senate and House of Representatives about their frustrations with the land grant confirmation process.

We, the undersigned, residents of the state of California, and some of us citizens of the United States, previously citizens of the Republic of Mexico, respectfully say: ...

That ... very few of the inhabitants of California opposed the [American] invasion; some of them welcomed the invaders with open arms; a great number of them acclaimed the new order with joy, giving a warm reception to their guests, for those inhabitants had maintained very feeble relations with the government of Mexico and had looked with envy upon the development, greatness, prosperity, and glory of the great northern republic, to which they were bound for reasons of commercial and personal interests, and also because its principles of freedom had won their friendliness.

When peace was established ... they immediately assumed the position of American citizens that was offered them, and since then have conducted themselves with zeal and faithfulness and with no less loyalty than those whose great fortune it was to be born under the flag of the North American republic—believing, thus, that all their rights were insured in the treaty, which declares that *their property shall be inviolably protected and insured*; seeing the realization of the promises made to them by United States officials; trusting and hoping to participate in the prosperity and happiness of the great nation of which they

From Robert Glass Cleland, *The Cattle on a Thousand Hills: Southern California, 1850–1880* (San Marino, Calif.: Huntington Library, 1975), 238–43.

now had come to be an integral part, and in which, if it was true that they now found the value of their possessions increased, that was also to be considered compensation for their sufferings and privations.

The inhabitants of California, having had no choice but to dedicate themselves to the rural and pastoral life and allied occupations, ignorant even of the laws of their own country, and without the assistance of lawyers (of whom there were so few in California) to advise them on legal matters, elected from among themselves their judges, who had no knowledge of the intricate technical terms of the law and who were, of course, incompetent and ill-fitted to occupy the delicate position of forensic judicature. Scattered as the population was over a large territory, they could hardly hope that the titles under which their ancestors held and preserved their lands, in many cases for over half a century, would be able to withstand a scrupulously critical examination before a court. They heard with dismay of the appointment, by Act of Congress, of a Commission with the right to examine all titles and confirm or disapprove them, as their judgment considered equitable. Though this honorable body has doubtless had the best interests of the state at heart, still it has brought about the most disastrous effects upon those who have the honor to subscribe their names to this petition, for, even though all landholders possessing titles under the Spanish or Mexican governments were not forced by the letter of the law to present them before the Commission for confirmation, nevertheless all those titles were at once considered doubtful, their origin questionable, and, as a result, worthless for confirmation by the Commission; all landholders were thus *compelled de facto* to submit their titles to the Commission for confirmation, under the alternative that, if they were not submitted, the lands would be considered public property.

The undersigned, ignorant, then, of the forms and proceedings of an American court of justice, were obliged to engage the services of American lawyers to present their claims, paying them enormous fees. Not having other means with which to meet those expenses but their lands, they were compelled to give up part of their property, in many cases as much as a fourth of it, and in other cases even more. . . .

The expenses of the new state government were great, and the money to pay for these was only to be derived from the tax on property, and there was little property in this new state but the above-mentioned lands. Onerous taxes were levied by new laws, and if these were not paid the property was put up for sale. Deprived as they were of the use of their lands, from which they had now no lucrative returns, the owners were compelled to mortgage them in order to assume the payment of taxes already due and constantly increasing. With such mortgages upon property greatly depreciated (because of its uncertain status), without crops or rents, the owners of those lands were not able to borrow money except at usurious rates of interest. The usual interest rate at that time was high, but with such securities it was exorbitant; and so they were forced either to sell or lose their lands; in fact, they were forced to borrow money even for the purchase of the bare necessities of life. Hoping that the Land Commission would take quick action in the revision of titles and thus relieve them from the state of penury in which they found themselves, they mortgaged their lands, paying compound interest at the rate of from three to ten per cent a month. The long-awaited relief would not arrive; action from the Commission was greatly delayed; and, even after the Commission would pronounce judgment on the titles, it was still necessary to pass through a rigorous ordeal in the District Court; and some cases are, even now, pending before the Supreme Court of the nation. And in spite of the *final* confirmation, too long a delay was experienced (in many cases it is still being experienced), awaiting the surveys to be made by the United States Surveyor-General. The general Congress overlooked making the necessary appropriations to that end, and the people were then obliged to face new taxes to pay for the surveys, or else wait even longer while undergoing the continued and exhausting demands of high and usurious taxes. Many persons assumed the payment of the surveyors and this act was cause for objection from Washington, the work of those surveyors rejected, and the patents refused, for the very reason that they themselves had paid for the surveys. More than 800 petitions were presented to the Land Commission, and already 10 years of delays have elapsed and only some 50 patents have been granted.

The petitioners, finding themselves unable to face such payments because of the rates of interest, taxes, and litigation expenses, as well as having to maintain their families, were compelled to sell, little by little, the greater part of their old possessions. Some, who at one time had been the richest landholders, today find themselves without a foot of ground, living as objects of charity—and even in sight of the many leagues of land which, with many a thousand head of cattle, they once had called their own; and those of us who, by means of strict economy and immense sacrifices, have been able to preserve a small portion of our property, have heard to our great dismay that new legal projects are being planned to keep us still longer in suspense, consuming, to the last iota, the property left us by our ancestors. Moreover, we see with deep pain that efforts are being made to induce those honorable bodies to pass laws authorizing *bills of review*, and other illegal proceedings, with a view to prolonging still further the litigation of our claims.

The manifest injustice of such an act must be clearly apparent to those honorable bodies when they consider that the native Californians were an agricultural people and that they have wished to continue so; but they have encountered the obstacle of the enterprising genius of the Americans, who have assumed possession of their lands, taken their cattle, and destroyed their woods, while the Californians have been thrown among those who were strangers to their language, customs, laws, and habits. . . .

The undersigned respectfully maintain that, if the promises and honor of the United States Government, so solemnly pledged, had been faithfully kept, Sonora, Baja California, and all the northern part of Mexico, seeing with envy the happy state of the Californians under their new government, would have been already anxiously clamoring to be admitted to the glorious confederation; but now, aware of the pitiful state in which the Californians find themselves, they adhere with almost frenzied despair to the feeble shadow of protection which they still enjoy under the confused, weak, and insecure government of unfortunate Mexico, looking forward with pain and dismay to an approaching conquest. . . .

Wherefore, the undersigned, with dignified obedience and respect to your sovereignty, beg, trust, and expect the justice and equity that should characterize such honorable bodies, by giving no consideration to, and refusing, not only the before-mentioned *bill of review*, but also any other demands from the state which, as at present, may tend to work injustice and cause the destruction of the rights of the old native Californians; but they should, on the contrary, respect, protect, and uphold the treaty of Guadalupe Hidalgo, by which conduct both the honor of your august bodies, and that of the general government of the United States as well, will be insured.

50

JUAN N. SEGUÍN

A Foreigner in My Native Land

1858

Juan Seguín, a native San Antonian who fought in the Texas War for Independence and eventually became mayor of his hometown, was forced to move to Mexico in 1842 after his allegiance to the Lone Star Republic was questioned. His belief that he had become a foreigner in his native land was emblematic of the experiences of other ethnic Mexicans in the Southwest.

A native of the city of San Antonio de Béxar, I embraced the cause of Texas at the sound of the first cannon which foretold her liberty, filled an honorable role within the ranks of the conquerors of San Jacinto, and was a member of the legislative body of the Republic. In the very land which in other times bestowed on me such bright and repeated evidences of trust and esteem, I now find myself exposed to the attacks of scribblers and personal enemies who, to serve *political purposes* and engender strife, falsify historical fact with which they are but imperfectly acquainted. I owe it to myself, my children and friends to answer them with a short but true exposition of my acts, from the beginning of my public career up to the time of the return of General [John E. Wool] from the Rio Grande with the Mexican forces, among which I was then serving.

I address myself to the American people, to that people impetuous as the whirlwind when aroused by the hypocritical clamors of designing men but just, impartial, and composed whenever men and facts are submitted to their judgment.

I have been the object of the hatred and passionate attacks of a few troublemakers who, for a time, ruled as masters over the poor and oppressed population of San Antonio. Harpy-like, ready to pounce on everything that attracted the notice of their rapacious avarice, I was an

From Jesús F. de la Teja, ed., *A Revolution Remembered: The Memoirs and Correspondence of Juan N. Seguín* (Austin, Tex.: State House Press, 1991), 73–74.

obstacle to the execution of their vile designs. They therefore leagued together to exasperate and ruin me, spread malignant calumnies against me, and made use of odious machinations to sully my honor and tarnish my well earned reputation.

A victim to the wickedness of a few men whose false pretenses were favored because of their origin and recent domination over the country, a foreigner in my native land, could I stoically be expected to endure their outrages and insults? Crushed by sorrow, convinced that only my death would satisfy my enemies, I sought shelter among those against whom I had fought. I separated from my country, parents, family, relatives and friends and, what was more, from the institutions on behalf of which I had drawn my sword with an earnest wish to see Texas free and happy. In that involuntary exile my only ambition was to devote my time, far from the tumult of war, to the support of my family who shared in my sad condition.

Fate, however, had not exhausted its cup of bitterness. Thrown into a prison in a foreign country, I had no alternatives left but to linger in a loathsome confinement or to accept military service.

On one hand, my wife and children, reduced to beggary and separated from me; on the other hand, to turn my arms against my own country. The alternatives were sad, the struggle of feelings violent. At last the father triumphed over the citizen; I seized a sword that pained my hand. (Who among my readers will not understand my situation?) I served Mexico; I served her loyally and faithfully. I was compelled to fight my own countrymen, but I was never guilty of the barbarous and unworthy deeds of which I am accused by my enemies.

Ere the tomb closes over me and my contemporaries, I wish to publicize this stormy period of my life. I do it for my friends as well as for my enemies. I challenge the latter to contest with facts the statements I am about to make, and I confidently leave the decision to those who witnessed the events.

51

FRANCISCO RAMÍREZ

California Hospitality

September 18, 1855

Born in 1837, Los Angeles native Francisco Ramírez witnessed the American conquest firsthand. Ramírez worked as a typesetter while a teenager and eventually became an editor for the Spanish-language section of the Los Angeles Star. *In 1855, with the* Star's *blessing, he launched* El Clamor Público, *which published articles written in Spanish and was committed to serving the Mexican population of California.* El Clamor Público *reported on and criticized the U.S. government and its citizens' treatment of native Californians. As Ramírez became more strident in his criticism of Americans, he lost financial backing for his newspaper, and it ceased publication in 1859. After moving briefly to Sonora, Mexico, Ramírez returned to Los Angeles, where he worked as a printer, postmaster, translator for the state, and editor for the short-lived Spanish-language newspaper* La Crónica. *He eventually moved to Ensenada, Baja California, where he had a successful law practice and was one of the city's leading citizens until his death in 1908.*

Who is the foreigner in California? He is what he is not in any other part of the world: he is what is not known even in the most inhospitable land. In speaking about this matter, we are particularly referring to the sons of the diverse countries of Hispanic America, the sons of those countries should be considered by the North Americans of California like brothers of the same family. Are these the same North Americans who claim to give us humanitarian lessons and take saving doctrines to our countries, to teach us how to govern ourselves, respect the laws, and maintain order, yet treat us worse than slaves in their own country? It is difficult to have to say it; however there are so many incidents that constantly confirm that the only answer to this question is yes. It is impossible not to come across a daily newspaper report that does not recount the boldest personal insult perpetrated

---

El Clamor Público, September 18, 1855, 1. Translated by Ernesto Chávez.

against a Mexican. The successive injustices that have occurred lately and that continue occurring every day are the most eloquent evidence of the way that the sons of Mexico, and in general all Hispanic people, are treated in California.

Killings, thefts, effronteries, and outrages of every kind, these are the exploits of many of the sons of North America. Our newspaper does not have the space to solely dedicate itself to publishing the occurrences that we hear about, and that the American newspapers publish, all of which are based on undeniable facts. Suffice to say that they reveal the most lamentable conditions for the sons of Mexico.

52

LOS ANGELES STAR

An Interview with Noted Bandit Tiburcio Vásquez
May 16, 1874

Tiburcio Vásquez was born in Monterey, California, into a middle-class family in 1835. His social standing guaranteed that he received a good education, and under different circumstances he would have become a prominent citizen. The American conquest, however, set his life on a different course. After shooting a constable in 1852, Vásquez turned to a life of crime. In an interview conducted after his capture in 1873, Vásquez explained the reasons for his actions.

My career grew out of the circumstances by which I was surrounded as I grew to manhood. I was in the habit of attending balls and parties given by the native Californians, into which the Americans, then beginning to become numerous, would force themselves and shove the native-born men aside, monopolizing the dances and the women. This was about 1852.

Los Angeles Star, May 16, 1874. Reprinted from Robert Glass Cleland, *The Cattle on the Thousand Hills: Southern California, 1850–1880* (San Marino, Calif.: Huntington Library, 1975), 274–79.

A spirit of hatred and revenge took possession of me. I had numerous fights in defense of what I believed to be my rights and those of my countrymen. The officers were continually in pursuit of me. I believed that we were unjustly and wrongfully deprived of the social rights which belonged to us. So perpetually was I involved in these difficulties that I at length determined to leave the thickly-settled portion of the country, and did so. . . .

. . . Robbery after robbery followed each other as rapidly as circumstances allowed, until in 1857 or '58 I was arrested in Los Angeles for horse-stealing, convicted of grand larceny, sent to the penitentiary and was taken to San Quentin and remained there until my term of imprisonment expired in 1863. . . .

After my discharge from San Quentin I returned to the house of my parents and endeavored to lead a peaceful and honest life. I was, however, soon accused of being a confederate of Procopio and one Sato, both noted bandits, the latter of whom was afterward killed by Sheriff Harry Morse of Alameda county. I was again forced to become a fugitive from the law-officers, and, driven to desperation, I left home and family and commenced robbing whenever opportunity offered. I made but little money by my exploits. I always managed to avoid arrest. I believe I owe my frequent escapes solely to my courage. I was always ready to fight whenever opportunity offered, but always tried to avoid bloodshed.

I know of nothing worthy of note until the Tres Pinos affair occurred. The true story of that transaction is as follows:

I, together with four other men, including Chavez, my lieutenant, and one Lava, who is now in jail at San Jose awaiting an opportunity to testify, he having turned state's evidence, camped within a short distance of Tres Pinos. I sent three of the party, Lava included, to that point, making Lava the captain. I instructed them to take a drink, examine the locality, acquaint themselves with the number of men around and wait until I came. I told them not to use any violence, as when I arrived I would be the judge, and if anybody had to be shot, I would do the shooting.

When I arrived there with Chavez, however, I found three dead men, and was told that two of them were killed by Lava, and one by another of the party named Romano; the rest of the men in the party were all tied. I told Lava and his companions that they had acted contrary to my orders; that I did not wish to remain there long. Lava and his men had not secured money enough for my purpose, and I told a woman, the wife of one of the men who was tied, that I would kill him if she did not procure funds. She did so, and we gathered up what goods and clothing and provisions we needed and started for Elizabeth Lake, Los Angeles county. On the way there I seduced the wife of the man Lava. He did not discover our intimacy until we had pitched camp at the lake. He at once rebelled and swore revenge. He left his wife at . . . Elizabeth Lake, and started to Los Angeles to deliver himself up, as well as to deliver me to the authorities, if he could do so. . . .

I went from there to a small settlement known as Panama. . . . It was well known to the citizens of Bakersfield, which is only two or three miles from Panama, that I was there, and arrangements were made for my capture; but the attack was not made until I had been gone 24 hours. Then they came and searched the house in which I was supposed to be concealed. When I left Panama I started for the Sweetwater Mountains and skirted their base, never traveling along the road, but keeping along in the direction of Lone Pine. I returned by the way of Coyote Holes, where the robbery of the stage took place. Here Chavez and myself captured the diligencia[1] and sixteen men. Chavez held his gun over them while I took their money and jewelry. We got about $200 and some pistols and jewelry, watches, etc., also a pocketbook belonging to a Mr. James Cray, containing about $10,000 worth of mining stock which I threw away. One man was disposed to show fight; and to preserve order, I shot him in the leg and made him sit down. I got six horses from the Stage Company, two from the station. I drove four of them off in one direction and went myself in another to elude pursuit.

I wandered around in the mountains after that until the time of the Repetto robbery. The day before this occurred I camped at the Piedra Gordo at the head of the Arroyo Seco. I had selected Repetto as a good subject. In pursuance of this plan I had adopted, I went to a sheep herder employed on the place and asked him if he had seen a brown horse which I had lost; inquired if Repetto was at home; took a look at the surroundings, and told the man I had to go to the Old Mission on some important business, and that if he would catch my horse I would give him $10 or $15. I then returned by a roundabout way to my camp on the Arroyo Seco. . . .

I found [Repetto] at home and told him I was an experienced sheepshearer, and asked him if he wished to employ any shearers; told him that my friends, the gentlemen who were waiting out by the fence were also good shearers and wanted work. All were invited in, and as they entered surrounded Repetto. I then told him that I wanted money. . . .

---

[1] *diligencia*: Stagecoach.

... He sent a messenger to the bank in Los Angeles for the money, being first warned that in the event of treachery or betrayal, his life would pay the forfeit.

The messenger returned, not without exciting the suspicions of the authorities, who, as is well known, endeavored at that time to effect my capture, but failed.

... After my escape I wandered for awhile in the mountains; was near enough to the parties who were searching for me to kill them if I had desired to do so.

For the past three weeks I have had my camp near the place where I was captured, only coming to the house at intervals to get a meal. I was not expecting company at the time the arrest was made, or the result might have been different.

53

JOURNAL OF COMMERCE
AND COMMERCIAL BULLETIN

This Is Our Manifest Destiny
November 24, 1897

The concept of manifest destiny lived on after the U.S. war with Mexico. It was most prominently resurrected in the 1890s when the United States engaged in new imperial ventures abroad, especially in Hawaii, as this article from the Journal of Commerce and Commercial Bulletin *makes clear. Note how the term* manifest destiny *is used here and what this reveals about the use of ideas and concepts in U.S. history.*

It is all very well for the Austrian Foreign Minister [Count Goluchowski] to appeal to Europe to band together against the terrible competition of the United States, but what are they going to do about it? We do not suppose that Europe is yet very seriously alarmed at our exports of manufactured goods, though these are increasing, and they

"Dread of American Competition," *Journal of Commerce and Commercial Bulletin,* November 24, 1897, 6.

may in years seriously threaten the factories of Europe. This is not a very good year to propose in Europe the exclusion of food from America. What would be the prices of bread and meat in Vienna if Europe succeeded in erecting a substantial barrier against trade with the United States? Hungary would not object to famine prices for flour, but Austria has to import food stuffs, as well as Germany, and France and England, though of course not in the ratio of the last named. Quite possibly the Austrian statesman looks forward to the time when American manufactured goods will press into all foreign markets, but what can a European union avail? It cannot prevent our manufactured goods from crowding those of Europe out of the markets of Asia and Africa and the Southern half of our continent, even if it keeps them out of the European continent. European nations might conceivably form themselves into a zollverein,[1] but that would seriously affect their revenues and it would not save their foreign trade. They might raise their tariffs against each other as well as against us, and so guard their home markets more rigidly and save their revenues, but it would only hasten the loss of their foreign trade to us, and all of them are dependent now upon their foreign trade, which they cannot protect from us.

The truth of the matter is, we apprehend, that Count Goluchowski has come to a better comprehension of the prospects of American competition than other European statesmen have reached. To intelligent and candid observers it has been long enough apparent that the United States have reached a point at which they must become far more important competitors for the world's commerce than they have hitherto been. Our development has attained a stage at which the national production must run upon manufactures in a much larger ratio than heretofore. With the most modern machinery, the best trained labor, the cheapest transportation, an ever increasing supply of capital seeking employment, and raw materials of every kind in abundance at our doors,—we have entered upon conditions of cheapness in production of the leading staples which are beginning to surpass those of the great commercial nations. The point has been passed at which tariffs can materially regulate domestic prices; we must, perforce[2] of our constantly increasing productive capacity, go on augmenting our output of goods beyond the limits of home consumption,

---

[1]*zollverein*: A union between certain states of the German empire for the maintenance of a uniform rate of customs duties from other countries and of free trade among themselves.

[2]*perforce*: By necessity.

and values must accommodate themselves to supply. This is our new status; this is our manifest destiny; and it means a cheapness that will open to us the markets of the world. Count Goluchowski has evidently caught a glimpse of this new drift of transatlantic commerce and foresees its outcome in transforming the United States from a customer into a competitor. At the same time, he is not unaware of the fiscal burdens attendant on the military policies of the European governments and of the simpler methods of this republic; and it is not surprising if his dreams trouble him. The vision of a great competition between the two continents is not a pleasant subject to brood upon. The Count will probably end by peacefully accepting the inevitable.

A Chronology of Events Related to the U.S.-Mexico War (1789–1897)

1789 U.S. Constitution ratified.

1790 Naturalization Act limits U.S. citizenship to whites only.

1795 Treaty of San Lorenzo negotiated between the United States and the Kingdom of Spain, establishing America's southern boundary.

1803 United States purchases the Louisiana Territory from France for $15 million.

1810 *September 16*: Mexican independence declared.

1819 United States purchases Florida from Spain through the Adams-Onís Treaty.

1821 Plan de Iguala issued, paving the way for Mexican independence.

Agustín de Iturbide declares himself emperor of Mexico.

Mexican government offers Moses Austin land grants in Texas. Austin dies before the pact can be completed, but his son Stephen follows through on the agreement, which allows him to take three hundred families to Texas.

1823 Agustín I abdicates.

1824 Mexican Constitution ratified.

1826 *December*: Republic of Fredonia uprising.

1828 General Manuel Mier y Terán heads a commission to investigate conditions in Texas.

1829 *September*: President Vicente Guerrero frees the slaves in Mexico.

1830 Indian Removal Act passed.

Mexican colonization law passed, outlawing American immigration to Texas.

1832 Antonio López de Santa Anna elected president of Mexico but decides not to assume office.

1833   *April*: Stephen Austin, Sam Houston, and fifty-five delegates from Texas meet in San Felipe de Austin to draft a constitution for a proposed "department" of Texas, which would become part of the Mexican republic.

1834   *May*: Santa Anna assumes the presidency and revokes the 1824 Mexican Constitution.

1835   *May*: Santa Anna defeats the Zacatecas army and leads the way to the overthrow of the federalist republic and its replacement with a centralist government.

   September: Texas War for Independence begins in Gonzales.

   November 3: Texan Consultation of Representatives establishes provisional government for a proposed department of Texas in the Mexican republic as a last-ditch effort to avoid war with Mexico.

   December 10: Santa Anna and his troops begin their march to Texas.

1836   *February 23*: Santa Anna and his troops reach San Antonio.

   March 2: Texan Consultation of Representatives meets at Washington-on-the-Brazos and adopts the Texas Declaration of Independence.

   March 6: Battle of the Alamo begins at 5:00 A.M.; by 6:30 A.M. the fighting ends, and the Texans are defeated.

   April 21: Santa Anna and his men are caught by surprise and defeated by an army led by Sam Houston at the San Jacinto River.

1837   *March 3*: United States recognizes Texas's independence, but due to potential sectional conflict, annexation is put on hold.

1838   Land Office for the Republic of Texas is established to investigate Spanish and Mexican land grant claims in areas that were part of the republic at its founding.

1839   International tribunal investigates American business claims against Mexico and awards the aggrieved parties $2 million of the $9 million requested. Mexico must take out loans to pay the claims, leading to further financial turmoil for the republic.

1842   *Summer*: Texan–Santa Fe expedition invades New Mexico but is soon defeated.

   Juan Seguín and twenty prominent families leave San Antonio after their loyalty to Texas is questioned, and they are harassed by Texas authorities.

   Fall: Lieutenant Thomas ap Catesby Jones, acting on a rumor of war between the United States and Mexico, seizes the Mexican fortress at Monterey, California. Although he apologizes for his mistake, his actions cause further Mexican distrust of Americans.

1844 *November*: James K. Polk elected president after pledging to re-annex Texas and reoccupy Oregon.

1845 *February*: A simple majority of both houses of Congress approves a resolution on Texas annexation.

Spring: Polk sends Envoy Extraordinaire and Minister Plenipotentiary John Slidell to Mexico to negotiate the Texas border dispute.

June: Texan Convention of Representatives approves the annexation resolution; Slidell returns to Mexico to attempt to buy New Mexico and California for $5 million and $25 million, respectively; Polk instructs General Zachary Taylor to move his army into Corpus Christi and approach the Rio Grande.

July: In a *Democratic Review* article supporting the annexation of Texas, John L. O'Sullivan uses the phrase "manifest destiny" for the first time.

October: People of Texas ratify the annexation measure; Polk orders Taylor to move his troops south of the Nueces River into what is clearly Mexican land.

December 29: Texas enters the Union.

1846 *January*: The United States sends an exploratory expedition under the command of John C. Frémont into California.

Mid-April: United States initiates a blockade of the Rio Grande; dispatches soldiers near New Mexico; and sends warships to the coast of Veracruz, Mexico, and ports in California.

April 12: Mexican commander Pedro de Ampudia informs Taylor that he must immediately retreat to the north side of the Nueces River and that failing to do so will be looked upon as an act of war; Taylor replies that he will not retreat and says that the responsibility for the hostilities to come will fall on Ampudia.

April 23: President Mariano Paredes y Arrillaga declares the initiation of a defensive war against the United States; sends General Mariano Arista, commander of the Army of the North, to Matamoros and orders him to attack the American forces.

April 25: Mexican army attacks the American troops at Rancho de Carricitos, located between the Nueces River and the Rio Grande, killing eleven dragoons and wounding five.

April 26: Taylor receives word of the battle and immediately sends news of the attack to Washington, D.C.

May 8: Battle of Palo Alto (Texas).

May 9: Battle of Resaca de la Palma (Texas); word of initial skirmish at Rancho de Carricitos reaches Washington.

May 11: Polk sends a message to Congress claiming that "Mexico has . . . shed American blood upon the American soil" and asking that war be declared on Mexico; Walt Whitman's editorial in the *Brooklyn Daily Eagle* calls for all-out aggression against Mexico.

May 13: An overwhelming majority of both houses of Congress approve war declaration.

June: Polk administration settles the Oregon dispute with Great Britain, agreeing to divide the territory at the forty-ninth parallel.

June 17: James Russell Lowell's satirical poem denouncing Massachusetts governor George Briggs's call for volunteers is published in the *Boston Courier*; this and other similar poems are eventually collected and published as *The Biglow Papers*. Also, at a Philadelphia mass meeting of women gathered to protest the war, Lucretia Mott reads a response to an address from British women in solidarity with their advocacy for peace.

July: Henry David Thoreau refuses to pay his taxes in protest against the war. His actions prompt him to write "Resistance to Civil Government," a lecture from which the essay "On Civil Disobedience" is derived.

July 4: Bear Flag Republic proclaimed in California.

July 7: Commodore John Drake Sloat captures Monterey, California.

August 8: Polk sends Congress a request for an additional $2 million to be used at his discretion in the war with Mexico; Pennsylvania congressman David Wilmot introduces his proviso to ban slavery in any territory acquired from Mexico; bill defeated in the Senate.

August 13: Commodore Robert F. Stockton occupies Los Angeles.

August 16: New Mexico governor Manuel Armijo disbands his troops and flees to Chihuahua.

August 18: Colonel Stephen Watts Kearny and his men march into Santa Fe.

September 20–24: Battle of Monterrey (Mexico).

September 25: Kearny and his men leave for California, which they reach two months later.

November 16: Taylor occupies Saltillo.

November 18: Polk appoints Major General Winfield Scott to lead an expedition to Veracruz.

December 6: Battle of San Pascual, the bloodiest conflict in California, fought near San Diego.

1847 *January 8*: Battle of San Gabriel (California).

January 10: Stockton reoccupies Los Angeles.

January 13: Treaty of Cahuenga signed, ending the fighting in California.

February 22–23: Battle of Buena Vista ends the fighting in northern Mexico.

March 9: American troops land below Veracruz.

March 29: Mexican troops surrender Veracruz.

April 8: Scott begins his advance into the interior of Mexico.

April 18: Battle of Cerro Gordo.

May 15: Advance party of Scott's army of occupation arrives in Puebla.

Early August: Five hundred new U.S. troops land in Mexico and soon arrive in Puebla.

August 7: Scott begins to move his men toward Mexico City.

August 19: Battle of Contreras.

August 20: Battle of Churubusco.

September 13: Battle of Chapultepec.

September 14: American troops occupy Mexico City.

September 16: Santa Anna relinquishes the presidency.

1848 *January 13*: Polk relieves Scott of his command.

January 24: Gold discovered in California. The following year's gold rush brings more than 100,000 miners to the state, ensuring the establishment of a new order in the former Mexican territory.

February 2: Treaty of Guadalupe Hidalgo signed by representatives of the U.S. and Mexican governments.

March 10: Treaty of Guadalupe Hidalgo ratified by the U.S. Senate.

May 26: Protocol of Querétaro, explaining the deletion of Article X of the Treaty of Guadalupe Hidalgo, agreed on by the U.S. and Mexican governments.

May 30: Treaty of Guadalupe Hidalgo ratified by Mexican Congress.

June 12: American troops evacuate Mexico City.

1850   *September 9*: California admitted to the Union.

California legislature institutes the Foreign Miners Tax, designed to protect Americans from competition from Mexican, Latin American, and Chinese miners. The legislation ensures that many native-born Californians (Californios) will be driven from mining.

1851   California Land Act, setting up a commission to investigate Spanish and Mexican land grants, passed by U.S. Congress. Eventually, the Land Grant Commission confirms 604 of the 816 claims it investigates, but claimants incur exorbitant legal costs, and many go bankrupt trying to save their land.

1853   Gadsden Treaty signed, giving the United States an additional 29,142,000 acres of Mexican territory in the present-day states of New Mexico and Arizona.

Congress appoints William Pelham to the office of surveyor general of New Mexico. Pelham is charged with investigating Spanish and Mexican land grants in New Mexico.

1855   Francisco Ramírez begins publishing the Spanish-language newspaper *El Clamor Público* in Los Angeles. It reports on the city's ethnic Mexican population and their disillusionment with the new American order.

1871   *Fall*: Tiburcio Vásquez and his men rob the Visalia, California, stagecoach. He soon gains a reputation as a desperado and bandit among U.S. authorities, while ethnic Mexicans view him as a hero waging war against an unjust American system. Two years later, after a series of robberies throughout the state, he is captured and executed in 1874.

1897   *Journal of Commerce and Commercial Bulletin* proclaims that manifest destiny will open the markets of the world to the United States.

Questions for Consideration

1. Contrast U.S. and Mexican perceptions of each other before and during the war.
2. Do you think the war was inevitable? Why or why not?
3. What does this historical moment reveal about the process of nation building?
4. What does it tell us about the social construction of citizenship and race? How are insiders and outsiders defined?
5. How did Mexico view America's westward expansion prior to the war?
6. What were the causes of the Texas revolution?
7. How would you characterize U.S.-Mexico diplomatic relations just before the war?
8. What were the motivating factors for the United States going to war with Mexico?
9. What role did slavery play in causing the war?
10. How would you characterize the American public's perception of the war?
11. How were popular representations of the war circulated in the United States?
12. What themes and issues do these popular representations highlight?
13. What were the views of U.S. soldiers involved in the war?
14. In general, how did the Mexican public view the war?
15. How did American women view the war?
16. How did Americans view Mexican women during the war?
17. What was the postwar era like for Mexican women?
18. Why would American leaders such as John C. Calhoun take a position that seemed counter to sectional interests?
19. What kinds of issues emerged at the end of the war concerning Mexico, its land, and its people?

20. What issues affecting Mexicans living in the conquered territories emerged at the end of the war?

21. What were some of the reactions of Mexicans to the loss of land and civil rights?

22. What were the short-range and long-range impacts of the war?

Selected Bibliography

Acuña, Rodolfo. *Occupied America: A History of Chicanos*. 6th ed. New York: Longman, 2007. A survey of Chicano history that presents the U.S. war with Mexico and its aftermath from an ethnic Mexican perspective. Acuña's extensive research in both primary and secondary sources makes this an essential sourcebook for anyone interested in the Mexican American past.

Alcaraz, Ramón, et al., eds. *The Other Side; or, Notes for the History of the War between Mexico and the United States*. Translated and edited by Albert C. Ramsey. New York: J. Wiley, 1850. Consisting of reminiscences of Mexican soldiers involved in the war, this volume gives detailed accounts of the conflict's various battles.

Bauer, K. Jack. *The Mexican War, 1846–1848*. New York: Macmillan, 1974. This military history of the Mexican War provides the most detailed coverage of military strategy, but it is dated in that it blames Mexico for the war.

Brack, Gene. *Mexico Views Manifest Destiny, 1821–1846: An Essay on the Origins of the Mexican War*. Albuquerque: University of New Mexico Press, 1975. Focusing on Mexico's reasons for going to war against the United States, newspapers serve as this study's research base. It argues that Mexicans were fearful of American racism and saw the war as a way to save their republic.

Christensen, Carol, and Thomas Christensen. *The U.S.-Mexican War*. San Francisco: Bay Books & Tapes, 1998. The companion book to the PBS Series *The U.S.-Mexican War, 1846–1848*, this volume is filled with pictures and maps. It presents a balanced view of the conflict and includes quotations throughout from both Americans and Mexicans. *The U.S.-Mexican War* is a good start for those who want a quick and popular approach to the conflict.

Connor, Seymour V., and Odie B. Faulk. *North America Divided: The Mexican War, 1846–1848*. New York: Oxford University Press, 1971. This book is tinged with racist language that degrades Mexicans and views their reasons for going to war as unrealistic. Its attribute lies in its extensive bibliography, which lists more than 760 books and pamphlets dealing with the conflict.

Eisenhower, John S. D. *So Far from God: The U.S. War with Mexico, 1846–1848*. New York: Random House, 1989. This popular account by a nonscholar blends military history with biography. Eisenhower focuses on the various people involved in the war—including James K. Polk, Winfield Scott, and Ulysses S. Grant—to provide a personal view of the conflict.

González, Deena J. *Refusing the Favor: The Spanish-Mexican Women of Santa Fe, 1820–1880*. New York: Oxford University Press, 1999. Focusing on the impact of the American conquest on women in New Mexico, González shows that while most women in Santa Fe lost honor and status following the U.S. takeover, some were able to resist domination and make the new order work for them.

Griswold del Castillo, Richard. *The Treaty of Guadalupe Hidalgo: A Legacy of Conflict*. Norman: University of Oklahoma Press, 1990. Examining the treaty that ended the U.S. war with Mexico, this book focuses on the framing of the accord as well as its political, economic, and social effects on ethnic Mexicans throughout the years.

Horsman, Reginald. *Race and Manifest Destiny: The Origins of American Racial Anglo-Saxonism*. Cambridge: Harvard University Press, 1981. A classic study that argues for the importance of racial thought in the war's origins and its aftermath. Ultimately, this book makes clear the centrality of race in U.S. history.

Johannsen, Robert W. *To the Halls of the Montezumas: The Mexican War in the American Imagination*. New York: Oxford University Press, 1985. Detailing the popular representations emerging from the U.S. war with Mexico, Johannsen provides incisive analysis that highlights the conflict's significance in U.S. history and shows that the mid-nineteenth-century American romantic impulse was intrinsically linked to imperial ventures.

McCaffrey, James M. *Army of Manifest Destiny: The American Soldier in the Mexican War, 1846–1848*. New York: New York University Press, 1992. A social history of soldiers in the war, *Army of Manifest Destiny* is concerned with the everyday experiences of the combatants and describes their emotions and attitudes about the conflict.

Montejano, David. *Anglos and Mexicans in the Making of Texas, 1836–1986*. Austin: University of Texas Press, 1987. An important study that reveals how both Anglos and Mexicans negotiated to form Texas. Montejano pays particular attention to the construction of race, ethnicity, and class in the Lone Star State.

Pitt, Leonard. *The Decline of the Californios: A Social History of the Spanish-Speaking Californians, 1846–1890*. Berkeley: University of California Press, 1966. This pioneering study looks at the aftermath of the U.S. war with Mexico and how the conflict affected the ethnic Mexicans in California. Though primarily concerned with the elite, it is vital to understanding the post-1848 era in general.

Reséndez, Andrés. *Changing National Identities and the Frontier: Texas and New Mexico, 1800–1850*. Cambridge: Cambridge University Press, 2004. Focusing on Mexico's northern frontier in the era before the U.S. war with Mexico, Reséndez reveals how the region's residents interacted with one another, the United States, and Mexico, and in so doing constructed identities that were on the margins of two nations.

Ruiz, Ramón Eduardo. *The Mexican War: Was It Manifest Destiny?* New York: Holt, Rinehart and Winston, 1963. Consisting of excerpts from contemporary and historical accounts of the conflict, this volume probes the war's origins and provides various perspectives that place the blame on either the United States or Mexico. Though an old collection, it does a good job of highlighting the views of past historians.

Schroeder, John H. *Mr. Polk's War: American Opposition and Dissent, 1846–1848*. Madison: University of Wisconsin Press, 1973. Focusing on President Polk's desire for war with Mexico and the opposition that ensued, this study reflects the concerns of the Vietnam War era and its influence on the writing of history. It is still the only book to deal with dissent during the U.S. war with Mexico and is therefore essential for understanding the conflict.

Singletary, Otis A. *The Mexican War*. Chicago: University of Chicago Press, 1960. Though more than forty years old, this is still the best brief account of the U.S. war with Mexico. Singletary concentrates on the war itself rather than its origins and aftermath, but his discussion of the behind-the-scenes intrigue and military strategy are concise and incisive.

Smith, Justin H. *The War with Mexico*. 2 vols. New York: Macmillan, 1919. Winner of the Pulitzer Prize for history in 1920, this book was the benchmark for the study of the U.S. war with Mexico from the time it was published through the 1970s. Smith's extensive research in both American and Mexican archives ensured its place in the conflict's historiography, yet it is full of racist and denigrating portrayals of Mexicans that ultimately reveal more about the writing of history, and the Progressive Era mind-set, than about the historical events themselves.

Stephanson, Anders. *Manifest Destiny: American Expansion and the Empire of Right*. New York: Hill and Wang, 1995. Linking manifest destiny to an older tradition of mission dating back to the Puritans, Stephanson shows how this idea has been present throughout U.S. history in various forms.

Streeby, Shelley. *American Sensations: Class, Empire, and the Production of Popular Culture*. Berkeley: University of California Press, 2002. Building on Johannsen's ideas, Streeby shows how a literature of sensation had a profound influence on the war and other nineteenth-century imperial ventures. *American Sensations* also makes clear that 1848 was a pivotal year in U.S. history, for it not only marked the attainment of an American empire, but with the acquisition of Mexican territory and its people, it also revealed the Republic's deep-seated racial and class dimensions.

Acknowledgments (continued from p. iv)

Document 10: Ohland Morton. With an Introduction by Eugene C. Barker. *Terán and Texas: A Chapter in Texas-Mexican Relations* (Austin: Texas State Historical Association, 1948), 99–101. Reprinted courtesy of Texas State Historical Association, Austin. All rights reserved.

Document 29: Stella M. Drumm, ed., *Down the Santa Fe Trail and into Mexico: The Diary of Susan Shelby Magoffin, 1846–1847*, reprinted with permission of Yale University Press.

Document 38: "Notes and Documents: The Citizens of New Mexico, Report to the President of Mexico." *New Mexico Historical Review*, Vol. 26, no. 1 (Jan. 1951): 73–75. Copyright © 1951 by the University of New Mexico Board of Regents. All rights reserved.

Document 39: Robert Ryal Miller, ed., *The Mexican War Journal and Letters of Ralph W. Kirkham* (College Station: Texas A&M University Press, 1991), 32–34.

Document 43: Reprinted with permission by the University of South Carolina Press.

Documents 45 and 46: From *The View of Chapultepec: Mexican Writers on the Mexican-American War,* by Cecil Robinson, editor. © 1987 The Arizona Board of Regents. Reprinted by permission of the University of Arizona Press.

Document 49: Reprinted with the permission of the Henry E. Huntington Library.

Index

161

"Treaty of Guadelupe Hidalgo," 120–23
"Treaty of San Lorenzo," 44–45
Tres Pinos affair, 141
Trist, Nicholas P., 25
Tula, Dona, 92
"Two-Million-Dollar Bill," 15, 76–77
Tyler, John, 12

Unitarians, 17
United States
American settlement in Texas, 5–7, 52–55
annexation of Texas by, viii, 12–13, 35–37, 64–65, 149
armies needed by, 72
citizenship, 3, 25–26, 45–46, 121–22
criticism of, 62–63
declaration of war against Mexico, 1, 14–15, 150
diplomatic relations with Mexico, 10–13, 73
expansionism of, 4–5, 24, 52–55, 62–63, 64–65, 118–20
France and, 45–46
grievances against Mexico, 73–75, 79, 81–83
Indians and, 3, 4–5, 26, 42–43, 147
Mexican concerns about, 52–55, 62–63
Mexican grievances against, 69–71
Northern boundary of, 45
popular opinion in, 16–19
ratification of Guadalupe Hidalgo Treaty by, 25–26, 128–30, 151
southern boundary, 13–14, 25, 33*n*4, 44
Spain and, 44
troops stationed in Texas, 13–14
Western boundary of, 45
United States Democratic Review, 2, 35
U.S. Congress
"California Land Act," 130–32
"Indian Removal Act," 42–43
"Naturalization Act," 35–37, 37–38
Polk's war message to, 73–75
U.S. Pacific Fleet, 12
U.S. Senate
peace treaty deliberations, 24, 25–26
petition from Californios to, 28, 133–36
ratification of peace treaty by, 25–26
U.S. war with Mexico. *See also* Guadalupe Hidalgo, Treaty of
armies needed for, 72

chronology, 147–52
conduct of, 19–24
declaration of war, 1, 14–15, 150
descriptions of, 61–62, 71–72, 104–10, 112–14
expansionism and, vii, 2
illustrated memoirs about, 105–7
manifest destiny and, 22, 35
military strategy, 19
newspaper coverage of, 16–17
opposition to, 17–19, 76–80, 84–90, 101–3
peace treaty, 23, 24–27, 128–30, 151
political parties and, 83
Polk's rationale for, 73–75
popular opinion about, 16–19
race and, vii, 2–3
religion and, 79–80
significance of, vii, 32, 33
slavery and, vii, 2, 16, 19, 32–33, 76–77
support for, 80–83
surrender of Mexico, 23
terminology, ix
women's opposition to, 17, 88–90, 150

Valencia, Genera, 67
Vallejo, Mariano G., 21
Van Buren, Martin, 11, 12
Vásquez, Tiburcio, 30, 31, 152
interview with, 140–43
Velasco, Treaty of, 9
Veracruz, 22, 151
Vicario de Quitana, Donna Maria, 94
Villa, Pancho, 34*n*8
violence
bandits, 30–31, 83, 140–43, 152
racism and, 30–31
"Virtues of Mexican Women, The" (American Officer), 93–95

War for Independence, Texas, 7–10
"War Message to Congress" (Polk), 73–75
"War with Mexico" (Whitman), 82–83
"War with Mexico, The" (Douglass), 78–80
Webster, Daniel, 12–13
"Admission of Texas, The," 64–65
Whig Party
opposition to war by, 15, 76–77, 83
peace treaty negotiations and, 24
slavery and, 78